INNOVATIVE MINDS

LINUS PAULING
INVESTIGATING THE MAGIC WITHIN

Victoria Sherrow

RSVP

**RAINTREE
STECK-VAUGHN**
P U B L I S H E R S
The Steck-Vaughn Company

Austin, Texas

Acknowledgments

The publisher would like to acknowledge James R. Sheats of Hewlett Packard Laboratories for his expert review of the manuscript.

Published by Raintree Steck-Vaughn Publishers, an imprint of Steck-Vaughn Company.

Series created by Blackbirch Graphics
Series Editor: Tanya Lee Stone
Editor: Lisa Clyde Nielsen
Associate Editor: Elizabeth M. Taylor
Production/Design Editor: Calico Harington

Raintree Steck-Vaughn Staff
Editors: Shirley Shalit, Kathy DeVico
Project Manager: Lyda Guz

Library of Congress Cataloging-in-Publication Data

Sherrow, Victoria.
    Linus Pauling: investigating the magic within / Victoria Sherrow.
        p.   cm. — (Innovative minds)
    Includes bibliographical references and index.
    Summary: Examines the life and accomplishments of scientist and humanitarian Linus Pauling, known for his work on vitamins and environmental safety.
    ISBN 0-8172-4400-X
    1. Pauling, Linus, 1901–1994—Juvenile literature. 2. Biochemists—United States—Biography—Juvenile literature. 3. Chemists—United States—Biography—Juvenile literature. 4. Social reformers—United States—Biography—Juvenile literature. [1. Pauling, Linus, 1901–1994.]   I. Title.
II. Series.
QP511.8.P37S48   1997
540'.92—dc20
[B]   96-20311
                                                                          CIP
                                                                           AC

Printed in the United States of America
1 2 3 4 5 6 7 8 9 0   LB   00 99 98 97 96

Table of Contents

Linus Pauling was one of the most important scientists of the twentieth century. His model-making technique was a major innovation.

"Entranced by Chemical Phenomena"

A college junior stood in the corner of the chemistry library poring over scientific journals. Though still a student himself in the year 1920, Linus Pauling was also a teacher. Professors in the chemistry department at Oregon State Agricultural College had been so impressed with Pauling's work during his freshman and sophomore years there that they had hired him to teach a course to other students. His "office" was a desk in the corner of the library.

When not preparing lessons or grading papers, Pauling enjoyed reading the new scientific journals that came to the library. It was in one of these journals that he encountered a remarkable idea that was to influence his research for more than 50 years. Professor Gilbert Newton Lewis of the University of California at Berkeley had proposed a new explanation for how atoms—tiny units that make up matter—join together to form molecules of different substances. (In living things, groups of atoms called molecules, in turn, make up cells. Cells are the basic building blocks of most forms of life.)

Like other chemistry students, Pauling had learned an older theory: that atoms are linked somewhat like a hook and eye connect to each other. However, as yet no one had any idea of what this link consisted of or how the kind of atoms could affect it. Professor Lewis, building on the very recent work of Danish scientist Niels Bohr, proposed that chemical bonds consisted of pairs of electrons shared by two atoms. (An electron is a negatively charged particle. It is found in the atom along with the nucleus, which is composed of positively charged protons and neutrons, which are particles with no charge.)

Intrigued, Pauling read more about the electron-pair bond, or covalent bond, as scientists called it. As he studied the subject, many possibilities suggested themselves. He could imagine how the electron pair might explain the way in which atoms are held together to form molecules. These molecules often have very different properties, or traits, even though the number and type of atoms present are the same or similar. The electron-pair bond, he believed, was a foundation that would lead to systematic study of structural chemistry (the study of how elements and substances are composed). He was fascinated by how chemical reactions create entirely different substances. He later told an interviewer: "I was simply entranced by chemical phenomena, by the reactions by which different substances disappear

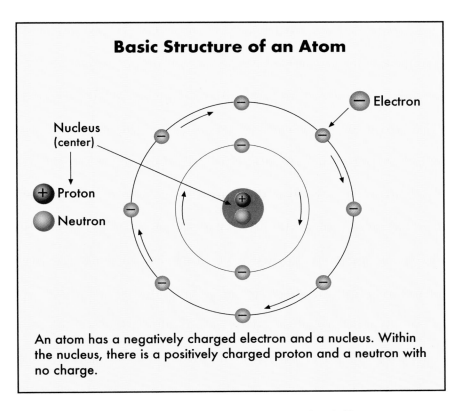

Basic Structure of an Atom

Nucleus (center)

+ Proton

Neutron

Electron

An atom has a negatively charged electron and a nucleus. Within the nucleus, there is a positively charged proton and a neutron with no charge.

and other substances, often with strikingly different properties, appear."

At that time, Linus Pauling began a quest that would lead to revolutionary discoveries in chemistry. His findings would strongly affect the fields of physics (the study of matter and energy) and biology (the study of living things). His urge to understand how the world was put together gave humankind a better understanding of the universe and of all kinds of cells. This research also paved the way for key gains in the fight against sickle-cell anemia and other diseases.

Linus Pauling was unique. Outspoken and energetic, he thought of an immense number of new ideas in his lifetime.

7

His interests and areas of expertise covered a broad range of science, but most revolved around the questions that he began asking during the time he read about the chemical bond: How are atoms and molecules put together? Why do molecules behave as they do? Can their behavior be predicted?

Outside the laboratory, Pauling distinguished himself as a social activist. Through the years, he crusaded for a number of social and political issues. He was particularly active in efforts to ban nuclear weapons and to stop nuclear testing that produced radiation hazardous to living things. Pauling would pay a high personal price for following his conscience, but he would also be recognized as a leader in the effort toward world peace.

Roots in the Northwest

Linus Carl Pauling overcame many obstacles to become one of the world's greatest scientists. He was born on February 28, 1901, in Portland, Oregon. Both sides of Linus Pauling's family had come West as pioneers. His maternal great-grandfather, Calvin Neal, was born in Tennessee in 1824. He traveled across country with a large train of covered wagons, arriving in Oregon in 1844. At that time, people came to the Northwest Territory to work in cattle drives and to build roads and bridges.

Calvin Neal's youngest daughter married Linus Wilson Darling, a small-town lawyer, who was Pauling's maternal grandfather. Linus Darling's father, William Allen Darling, had abandoned his family when he left to serve in the Union Army during the Civil War (1861–1865). Linus Darling himself was left alone when he was only 11 years old and his mother died. He became a "bound boy"—one obligated to work for a family in exchange for his keep. After being mistreated, Linus Darling ran away to fend for himself. He had no formal education, but he still learned to read and write. He became a teacher and then a land surveyor and postmaster. After that, he worked in a law office and studied the law until he was qualified to practice. The intelligence, spunk, and determination of Linus Darling were qualities that his grandson Linus Pauling would one day possess in large measure.

Along with some conventional people, this family included more unusual members: Linus Wilson Darling's brother Will was a painter and spiritualist who claimed to be in touch with a dead Indian. Stella Darling, Linus Pauling's aunt, was rumored to have once been a safecracker.

In May 1900, one of Linus Darling's daughters, Lucy Isabelle, called "Belle," wed a druggist and salesman named Herman W. Pauling. His parents were German immigrants. Belle and Herman would eventually have three children: Linus in 1901, followed by Pauline in 1902, and Frances Lucille in 1904. Herman worked hard to make ends meet, setting up a drugstore in Oswego, Oregon. There the family lived in a one-room tenement apartment near the Chinese section of town. When Herman could not make a living in Oswego, they moved to Condon, where Belle's family lived. Belle's father was not well-off, but he was still more prosperous than the young couple.

In Condon, Herman opened another drugstore. In those days, druggists did much more than prepare and sell drugs and health-care materials. Townspeople might also turn to them for first aid and medical help. Herman, like other druggists, probably even visited sick customers at their homes.

9

GROWING UP

It was in Condon, Oregon, that Linus started school at age five. He first attended a one-room schoolhouse. Early pictures of Pauling show a blond, curly haired boy with large, beautiful eyes. As a child, Linus often played with his cousin Mervyn Stephenson, who was three years older. He also spent hours visiting his father at the drugstore. Rows of liquids and powders sat in bottles on the shelves of the back room. Here Herman Pauling mixed such concoctions as Dr. Pfunder's Oregon Blood Purifier, which sold for 25 cents and was advertised in the local newspaper, *The Condon Globe*. Those shelves full of bottles must have fascinated young "Liney," as the family called him. Later, as a world-famous scientist, he would do groundbreaking work in the field of blood chemistry. By that time, medicine had gone well beyond the era of the "blood purifier" that Linus knew in his youth.

Young Linus also found plenty to do outdoors in this region of Oregon. Timberlands, streams, and fertile farmland surrounded the towns and cities. Linus's uncle, Herbert Stephenson, who was married to Belle's sister Goldie, owned a wheat farm. Linus liked to go there to visit his cousin Mervyn. The boys helped out on the farm by doing various chores. They went hunting, fishing, and swimming in their leisure time. Linus liked to hike, something that he would continue to love as an adult.

When Linus was about nine years old, the family moved back to Portland, again in the hope that Herman could earn more in his drugstore business. By this time, Linus had already shown some interest in science. He later recalled that he had conducted an "experiment" by mixing some powder in a laboratory that he had set up in the basement, then sprinkling the powder on a streetcar track. When the streetcar ran over it, the powder produced a small explosion. This was just one of the many experiments that young Linus tried. He often mixed and tested various chemicals just to see what would happen. On occasion, strange and sometimes awful odors would waft up from the basement, the result of yet another experiment.

In addition to his scientific explorations, Linus was an avid reader, devouring whatever books he could borrow from family members or friends. Two such books, each hundreds of pages long, came from his father's drugstore. They dealt with various illnesses and injuries and described the uses of drugs and the applications of medical treatments. These books may have spurred his interest in the workings of the human body.

Always interested in a wide variety of topics, Linus also began to read classic literature. At that time, public libraries were not yet common, and there were none near the Paulings' home. Impressed by his son's obvious intellectual gifts, Herman Pauling wrote a letter to *The Oregonian*, a local newspaper, saying that his son seemed talented. Herman asked for help in selecting books to stimulate Linus's intellectual abilities. But, sadly, he soon would not be alive to watch his son's progress and help him.

During this time, Herman was working long hours in his store, and his health was failing. In 1910, Herman Pauling died from a stomach illness; he was only 33 years old. Because the family was in Portland then, Linus not only grieved for his father but also missed Mervyn and his other friends. Widowed, and with three young children to raise,

Belle Pauling began running a rooming house, taking in boarders to earn money. Even so, the family could barely survive with these meager earnings. Belle was in poor health as well. To help earn money, Linus got a job setting up pins in a bowling alley. This was just the first of many jobs that the young Pauling would hold over the years.

AN EAGER STUDENT

Because his father's drugstore workshop no longer existed, Linus spent a great deal of time alone, reading and studying science. It was hard to find quiet places in the often noisy boardinghouse, which served mostly working men. At one point, Linus put a lock on his door for privacy.

Despite his father's death and his mother's lack of time to help, Pauling kept learning on his own. He found ways to explore science and other things that interested him. By seeking out books and people who could help him learn, he expanded his world. As Frances Lucille Pauling would later say of her brother, "Linus was always thinking."

Around age 11 or 12, Linus assembled a collection of insects, placing them in jars and labeling them based on information he found in a book. He also became interested in minerals. There were few minerals to examine near his home, but Linus's family was then traveling each Sunday, by steam train, to the home of his paternal grandparents. Charles and Adelheit Pauling lived in rural Oswego. Once in the countryside, Linus could find specimens for his collection.

Other learning opportunities came to Linus through a man named Yokum. As a "mountain man," Yokum had led an adventurous life during the U.S. expansion westward in the 1800s. He had trapped beavers for the fur trade and guided settlers through the wilderness on their journey west. Linus regularly stopped by Yokum's house while walking home from school. Yokum knew the Greek language and thought that Linus should learn it if he wanted to become a real scholar. He found an eager pupil in Linus. Yokum had a part-time job in a chemistry laboratory. He was able to bring Linus discarded equipment and supplies that the lab did not want.

When he began high school, Linus had another stroke of good fortune: He entered the class of an outstanding science teacher named Pauline Gabelle. At Smith College in Massachusetts, Gabelle had been a chemistry student—an unusual choice of subject major for a woman of that era. Linus highly respected Pauline Gabelle, a feeling he reserved for only a few people.

Gabelle taught general science and conducted innovative experiments in the classroom to bring the subject alive for her students. In addition, she showed them her fine collection of minerals, as they discussed how such substances had developed in the earth over time. Linus had been interested in minerals for some time. He built on the new knowledge that he gained in the class by adding to his own mineral collection. He also enjoyed examining the structure of these materials in the school's lab.

As a high school student, Linus also discovered an abandoned laboratory at the Oregon Iron and Steel Company. It was filled with old bottles of chemicals that were sitting unused. His grandfather Charles Pauling was a nightwatchman there, and he let Linus in to poke around. This was how Linus was able to supply himself with chemicals.

As he became more and more confident of his mental ability, Linus Pauling was developing a self-confidence that some people perceived as arrogance. He gravitated toward one close friend, Lloyd Jeffress, and a few students whom he viewed as his intellectual equals. Their talk usually focused on science, books, music, politics, or philosophy. Linus and Lloyd often played chess.

COLLEGE BOUND

During this period, Linus's family continued to struggle financially. To help out, he and his sisters held a number of outside jobs as well as doing household chores. During high school, Linus held a variety of jobs. He delivered milk, operated the film projector in a movie theater, and was a shipyard laborer on the Willamette River. At age 16, he tried working as a photographer's assistant, then attempted to run a photography business of his own, without success. As the end of Linus's high school years drew near, Belle Pauling looked forward to a time when her son could take a full-time job and really improve the family finances.

But Linus had other ideas. He was headed in a different direction, a direction that he had decided on several years earlier: He was going to college. And he was determined to become a scientist.

After high school, while waiting to hear whether he had been accepted at Oregon State Agricultural College (now Oregon State University), Pauling worked in a machine shop run by a German immigrant, Mr. Schweizerhoff. His wages were now equal to those of a grown man, which helped his family a great deal. Schweizerhoff encouraged

High School "Dropout"

Linus Pauling may well be the only person in history to receive his high school diploma (in 1962, at age 61!) *after* being awarded two Nobel prizes. This unusual situation came about because of a decision that he made during his last year of high school.

Pauling was fortunate that Washington High School was better than the average school in the region. He had access to courses in Latin and advanced mathematics, along with the courses in English, history, math, and science that all students were required to take. During his junior year, his chemistry teacher saw that Linus was an exceptional student. He let Linus conduct experiments in the laboratory after school. Linus also worked in the laboratory that he had set up at home.

Yet, although he was an outstanding student, Linus Pauling did not receive his high school diploma. In order to graduate officially from Washington High, he was required to take two courses in American history and civics. He had left these until the end of his senior year. At that time, though, Pauling was told that he could take only one of these courses at a time, which meant that he would have to remain in high school the next year. The school refused to make an exception in his case.

In the end, Pauling decided not to take the two courses at all. Instead, he took college-level algebra and trigonometry. In June 1917, he left high school without graduating. In 1962, Washington High granted the long-delayed diploma to its most famous alumnus.

Linus to pursue his dreams, telling him that he would be successful at whatever he attempted.

As Linus discussed his plans to leave the machine shop and go to college, a conflict erupted with his mother. He tried to explain why he must continue to study, while she begged him to reconsider. His two younger sisters, Pauline and Frances Lucille, were still living at home, said Belle, and besides, none of their friends or neighbors were going to college.

But Pauling held firm. He waited eagerly for the letter from Oregon State Agricultural College that would enable him to pursue his dream. That letter of acceptance finally came in mid-September 1917.

Of course, being accepted was one thing, but finding the money to pay for college was another. Supporting himself and paying for his books and college fees would be entirely up to Linus. He would also have to send whatever money he could spare home to his family.

Linus Pauling, nevertheless, was filled with enthusiasm and hope as he prepared for his journey to college in October 1917. He planned to be an engineering major. At that time, studying engineering was an important route by which people entered the field of science. Pauling boarded a train for the five-hour journey to Corvallis, Oregon, excited about what lay ahead. He was now one step closer to becoming a scientist.

From College

Student to

Professor

Linus Pauling entered Oregon State Agricultural College in Corvallis in 1917. Though he hadn't graduated, the college had accepted the number of high school credits he had accumulated. His performance in math and science had been outstanding, and the college could apparently be flexible in such matters in those days. He moved into an inexpensive rooming house where meals were served. In order to save money, Pauling planned to eat only one hot meal a day. But he knew that no matter how carefully he watched his money, his savings would last only a few months. So, besides enrolling for his engineering, chemistry, and mathematics courses, Pauling looked for work. He found a job in the girls' dormitory chopping wood, helping in the kitchen, mopping floors, and doing other odd jobs. It was hard work, and Pauling put in about 100 hours a month.

Oregon State Agricultural College was a state-supported school. Fortunately, tuition and registration fees were low, and books were not very costly. Most of Pauling's fellow students were not wealthy either.

BALANCING SCHOOL AND WORK

With his quick mind and strong educational background, Pauling was able to excel during his first year at college. Without much effort, he impressed teachers and students alike. Between his job and his schoolwork, he had little time left over for campus activities as a freshman. He had a few dates but was not known as being very outgoing or sociable.

While in college, Pauling continued to display the confidence in his own opinions and intellect that had emerged earlier in high school. He did not hesitate to correct or challenge professors if he thought they were wrong. He also developed a reputation as a skillful teacher himself, tutoring students who were having trouble with their chemistry assignments. He had the ability to explain difficult concepts in a clear and logical way—a skill that he would display later in life as a professor and lecturer.

Since World War I had begun in Europe in 1914, male students at American colleges were being prepared for possible military service. In 1918, after his freshman year, Pauling and some fellow classmates spent time in the Students' Army Training Corps.

When the program ended, Pauling went with his cousin Mervyn to work in the shipyards outside Corvallis. He also worked as a paving inspector that year. New blacktop highways were being built over the mountainous terrain across the state. As an inspector, Pauling collected samples of the materials used on the roads and analyzed them in a state-run chemical laboratory. Besides having a chance to carry out work related to his studies, Pauling enjoyed the chance to read scientific books in the lab.

By this time, Pauling had reached his full height of six feet. He spent quite a bit of time doing physical work. The lanky Oregonian developed a fairly athletic build and took gymnastics courses to strengthen his muscles. In his last years of college, he also joined the track team.

Pauling's sophomore year at college was a difficult one. His mother had become very ill with pernicious anemia, a disease of the blood that was then incurable. More money than ever was needed at home. Holding several jobs, Pauling often had to skip classes. He had little time to study and no time for any other activities.

The next summer, he returned to his job as a paving inspector. He sent home all of his pay so that his mother could save it in the bank for his college expenses. She used the money for the family's daily needs, however. That fall, Pauling realized that he could not afford to return to college for his junior year. He also found that his mother was becoming sicker, and he feared that she might die soon.

EXCITING NEW THEORIES

Having recognized his exceptional potential, the college made Pauling an employment offer in November that enabled him to return to school. He could earn $100 a year by teaching and assisting in laboratory work for the chemistry course that he had taken the year before. It was during this time that Pauling was able to explore many new books and the journals that contained the latest theories about the electron bond, or chemical bond—the manner in which atoms are linked.

The Structure of Water

Chemical bond

Two hydrogen atoms and one oxygen atom bond to form one molecule of water by sharing electrons. (This diagram does not show the true way in which electrons orbit the nuclei of atoms, but illustrates the sharing of electrons between atoms; the shared electrons orbit around both nuclei instead of just one.)

Gilbert Newton Lewis, a physical chemist, explained his thinking in a book about how atoms—those tiny particles that make up all substances—are joined together to form molecules. An example of a simple molecule is water: two hydrogen atoms connected to one atom of oxygen. Atoms join together in certain ways as a result of their "valence"— their negative or positive charge. Valence depends on the number of electrons in an atom and the manner in which they are arranged.

Besides Lewis's work, Pauling read some writing by Irving Langmuir, in which the famous American chemist discussed his ideas about shared electron pair bonds. The electrons can be mutually held by more than one atom at a time, Langmuir explained. One might compare this to a situation in which two horses are both hitched to two different wagons, which means that the wagons are also, essentially, attached to each other.

As he learned more about these new views of chemical bonding, Pauling became more critical of the old hook-and-eye theory, which maintained that atoms combine to form molecules because of the way they "fit" together according to some mechanical shape. The desire to understand chemical bonds gave Pauling an even stronger sense of direction for the future.

Happy Times

During his last two years of college, Pauling blossomed in new ways. He tackled more advanced mathematics and chemistry courses. In his junior year, he found physical chemistry class especially challenging. In fact, at times, he turned in assignments late because he could not figure out the answers.

That year, he also studied metallurgy—the science and technology of metals. In addition, Pauling became interested in crystallography, the study of crystals. Figuring out the nature of the molecules in crystals and how they are linked was to become one of Pauling's passions. He would spend years determining the patterns of different crystals, which are all variations of regular, polygon shapes.

Pauling blossomed in other ways during this period. He achieved the rank of cadet lieutenant after passing an examination given during the student officer-training program. Pauling also did well enough to be accepted into Scabbard and Blade, a military honor society. He joined the Greek letter fraternity, Delta Upsilon. And, although he had not been considered an outgoing person, Pauling now showed his skills as a speaker; he tied for second place in a college oratorical contest.

During his senior year, Pauling's personal life took a romantic turn: He met his future wife. Ava Helen Miller was a home economics major, and Pauling had agreed to teach the chemistry course for that class. As he began his first day as an instructor, Pauling asked a question about ammonium hydroxide, a chemical compound. Spotting a name on the class roster that was easy to pronouce, he directed his question to "Miss Miller." Pauling was impressed by Ava Helen's answer. His interest deepened as she showed a keen intelligence in class—sometimes in the process of questioning one of his ideas.

Within just a few weeks, the two were sharing long walks. Through their many conversations, they discovered that they had a number of experiences and ideals in common.

Dark-haired, petite Ava Helen Miller had been born into a middle-class Oregon family. Her widowed mother had managed to rear 12 children on a small farm. Ava Helen's sisters later said that they thought Linus was good-looking. Their mother also expressed approval.

Planning for the Future

As Pauling prepared to graduate, he faced many important decisions. He and Ava Helen wanted to marry, and he was determined to go on to graduate school and earn his doctorate. Yet his mother, who was now quite ill, wanted him to return home and teach in a high school there in order to support the family. Again, he insisted that he must continue his studies. An excellent education would enable him to do more for the family in the long run, he believed.

Knowing that Gilbert Lewis headed the chemistry department at the University of California at Berkeley, Pauling sent an application to the graduate school there. He also applied to prestigious Harvard University, near Boston, Massachusetts, although he did not think that he would like the New England winters or living so far away from Oregon. His third application went to a relatively new school, the California Institute of Technology (Caltech) in Pasadena. The programs there were being developed under the guidance of a top scientist, Arthur A. Noyes. Thus, students at Caltech might have more opportunities to shape their education and research than they would in a long-established place like Harvard. In addition, attracted by Noyes, fine research facilities, and the sunny climate, an excellent faculty was gathering at Caltech.

ARRIVAL AT CALTECH

Pauling received his Bachelor of Science (B.S.) degree in chemical engineering in 1922. Harvard had not offered enough financial aid for him to go there. The University of California at Berkeley did not respond soon enough. Caltech, however, made him an attractive offer of a teaching fellowship: By teaching just one course a semester in freshman chemistry, he could earn enough money to support himself. Pauling decided on Caltech.

Ava Helen stayed at Oregon State, where she had begun her sophomore year. Pauling could not afford to travel back and forth to see her, so the two exchanged many long letters. They hoped to marry the next June.

One of the highlights of studying at Caltech was that nine faculty members were available to work with just seven graduate students. The prominent American chemist and physicist Richard C. Tolman was at Caltech, along with Robert A. Millikan, another American and a Nobel prize–winning physicist.

Roscoe Dickinson, Pauling's graduate school adviser, was also from the United States. Dickinson was known for his outstanding work in the field of X-ray crystallography, an exciting technique that produces an image of molecules in crystal form, using X-ray diffraction.

In X-ray diffraction, scientists aimed X rays through slides containing samples of crystallized molecules, then let the rays fall onto photographic film. The resulting images could be analyzed to learn the structure of the molecules. X rays are a form of electromagnetic radiation, like light. The separation of white light into colors by a prism or in a rainbow is

Nobel prize-winning physicist Robert Millikan, shown here with his device for testing cosmic rays, was one of the faculty members with whom Pauling worked at Caltech.

a familiar example of diffraction. Because the wavelength of X rays is much shorter than that of visible light, and because it is comparable to the distance between atoms, the diffraction patterns of X rays are related to the spacings within atoms. With Dickinson's help, Pauling learned how to interpret photos made with this technique, calculating the distances between atoms and the angles of the chemical bonds that unite them.

While Pauling was in graduate school, he and Dickinson used X-ray diffraction techniques to examine various inorganic substances (substances that do not contain the elements carbon and hydrogen). Dickinson attempted to apply quantum mechanics—a branch of physics that explains the behavior of atomic particles—to his study of the chemical bond. He had learned about these concepts in England, where he had studied with chemist William L. Bragg at the famous Cavendish Laboratory. Bragg was one of the scientists who had developed the techniques of X-ray crystallography.

The laws of quantum mechanics had given scientists new ways to look at many physical phenomena. Before 1905, most scientists had viewed motion as continuous and thought that light waves were emitted in continuous streams. But that year, building on the work of others, German physicist Max Planck developed the revolutionary and controversial hypothesis that light was, instead, emitted in separate bundles, or "quanta," of energy. During the years when Pauling was going through graduate school, the theories of quantum, or wave, mechanics were being expanded, clarified, and debated. This was being done by such important scientists as the Dane Niels Bohr; the American Arthur H. Compton; the Germans Werner

Heisenberg, Wolfgang Pauli, Albert Einstein, and Max Born; the Austrian Erwin Schrödinger; and Louis de Broglie of France. And from his professor Richard Tolman, Pauling was hearing about ways in which principles of physics could be used in the study of chemistry.

At the end of his first year at the California Institute of Technology, in June 1923, Pauling packed his things into the old Ford that he had bought for $25 and hurried up to Oregon. He and Ava Helen were married at the home of one of her sisters.

Pauling had been granted some additional financial aid from Caltech, but he still needed extra money to support his two sisters, so he spent that summer working as a paving inspector. He then returned to Caltech, this time with his 19-year-old wife. The couple settled into a small apartment near the school.

GRADUATION AND FATHERHOOD

For two more years, Linus Pauling worked and studied, preparing his dissertation—the long research paper required for his doctoral degree. During his time at Caltech, he had been publishing scientific papers based on his studies of the atomic structure of crystals. These studies became the foundation of his dissertation. Linus Pauling received his doctorate in physical chemistry from Caltech in 1925, being granted the Doctor of Philosophy (Ph.D.) degree with high honors.

The Paulings had another reason to celebrate: They had just had their first child. A son they named Linus, Jr., was born in March 1925.

Now, Dr. Linus Pauling was ready to assume his role as a scientist. The 1920s were a very exciting time for science, especially in the study of molecules. New discoveries seemed to take place regularly in physics, as the foundations of classical mechanics were shaken to the core by the development of quantum mechanics. People continued to debate Albert Einstein's special theory of relativity, which he had stated in 1905, while he was already moving on to his more controversial and difficult-to-prove general theory of relativity. In the field of biology, the American Thomas Hunt Morgan and his colleagues were conducting exciting new studies of heredity. They experimented with the genes—the

Scientist Thomas Hunt Morgan made key discoveries in genetics during the early part of the twentieth century.

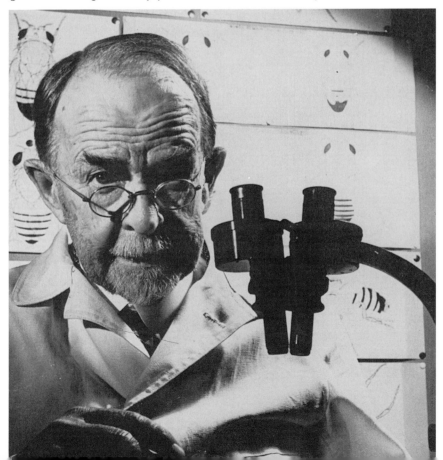

parts of the cell nuclei (or centers) that carry hereditary traits—of fruit flies.

As he delved into the structure of molecules, Pauling would join the ranks of scientists attempting to make key connections between physics and chemistry. He would make significant contributions to the developing field of molecular biology—the study of the cells of living organisms at the molecular level.

Pauling became convinced that he must do postgraduate study at some of the great scientific centers in Europe. He particularly wanted to work with the famous physicist Arnold Sommerfield at the University of Munich in Germany. The men had exchanged letters during the previous year, and Pauling had asked if he might spend time at Sommerfield's laboratory. In February 1926, his hopes were realized: He was one of 35 people who had been awarded the prestigious Guggenheim Fellowship, allowing him to study abroad.

Ava Helen arranged for their infant son, Linus, Jr., to stay with her mother in Oregon while the Paulings were traveling in Europe. She and her mother thought he was too young to make the trip. Besides, the young couple's funds were too limited to take him along. While many good things happened to the Paulings in 1926, sadly, that year Linus's mother, Belle, died.

A BLOSSOMING CAREER

In Munich, where he worked with Sommerfield, Pauling gained new insights into quantum theories and crystal structure. It was there that Pauling made his first quantum mechanical calculation of the structure of a molecule. The

PROFESSOR PAULING

Called the "boy professor" because he looked so young, Dr. Linus Pauling was a man who did not hesitate to show his individualism. He sometimes wore bright printed shirts and colorful sports clothing while teaching classes, in contrast to the dark, somber suits that were worn by other professors.

His personality could also be exuberant. Pauling's students found him a lively and creative teacher with a ready grin.

Pauling had an enthusiasm for teaching. In order to make difficult concepts more understandable to his freshman students, Pauling made models of molecules, cutting pieces of paper into geometric shapes and attaching them to wire frames. Pauling also constructed models from colorful plastic bubbles—what students came to refer to as his "baby toys." Using pieces of plastic tubes, he connected these balls together to make "molecules."

Although they were much larger than real molecules—which are millions of times smaller than the head of a pin—the models that he constructed enabled Professor Pauling to demonstrate for his students important facts about the atoms in different molecules. For example, he could show their relative size and their placement in relationship to one another. In later years, model-making would play an important role in some of Pauling's major discoveries, such as the structure of proteins.

His model-making helped other researchers as well. Scientists James D. Watson and Francis Crick credited Pauling with giving them the idea of constructing three-dimensional molecular models. This team was working on discovering the structure of the DNA molecule (DNA—deoxyribonucleic acid—is the substance that composes genes). In 1951, Watson suggested to Crick that they try model-making, the practical approach popularized by Pauling. Crick, who had read some of Pauling's articles and his book on chemical bonding, agreed. Watson and Crick (with Maurice Wilkins) later received the Nobel Prize for Medicine for their work.

Pauling was the youngest member of the Caltech
faculty when he became an assistant professor
there in 1927. This photo was taken in 1931.

insights he gained were fundamental to his later work on more complex systems and to a concept that he would develop called "resonance." Next, he spent time at Niels Bohr's institute in Copenhagen, Denmark. He attended lectures in Zurich, Switzerland, given by Erwin Schrödinger and other famous scientists. Schrödinger, a pioneer in quantum theories, later wrote the highly influential book *What Is Life?*

Meanwhile, Caltech was determined not to lose Linus Pauling. Arthur Noyes wrote to him in Europe, offering an assistant professorship. If he accepted, Pauling would become, at age 26, the youngest faculty member at Caltech. By now, the Paulings had been gone for more than a year, and Ava Helen was quite eager to return home to be with her young son. Pauling accepted the position, and they boarded a ship for America.

Back in Pasadena, the Paulings found a modest home to rent and settled into their new life. Although Pauling's mother had died in 1926, he continued to help his sisters financially.

In 1927, Pauling assumed his new position as assistant professor of chemistry at Caltech. He was somewhat disappointed, however. He had hoped that he would receive a joint appointment, in both physics and chemistry. But he got down to work, organizing his laboratory and preparing his lesson plans. The Gates Chemistry Laboratory at Caltech was being expanded, which meant that Pauling would soon have more room in which to work.

As he moved forward in his dual roles as innovative teacher and careful researcher, Linus Pauling embarked on one of the most exciting and most productive periods of his long career.

"The Nature of the Chemical Bond"

The year after Linus Pauling became a professor, he published his most significant paper to date. It dealt with an aspect of chemical bonding called "orbital hybridization." In the paper, Pauling sought to resolve a long-standing conflict over the nature of bonds formed by carbon. This was important because carbon is part of every organic substance.

As in other atoms, the electrons in a carbon atom move around the nucleus in waves. These electron waves are called "orbitals." The orbitals take different shapes. In carbon, three of the orbitals take the form of a figure-eight, while one is spherical.

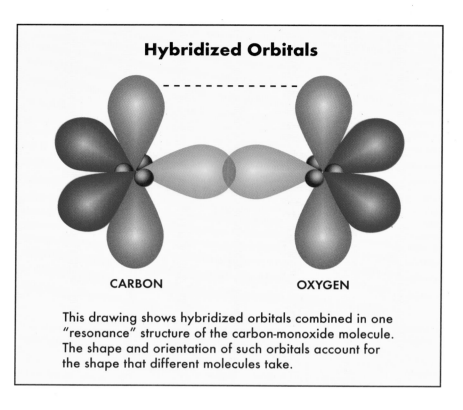

Hybridized Orbitals

CARBON   **OXYGEN**

This drawing shows hybridized orbitals combined in one "resonance" structure of the carbon-monoxide molecule. The shape and orientation of such orbitals account for the shape that different molecules take.

Pauling devised a mathematical procedure for combining the two types of orbitals into a single type. This is called "hybridization." Through hybridization of orbitals, Pauling said, the carbon atom could join, or bond, with atoms of different substances in a variety of ways.

With this concept, one could also understand why carbon-carbon bonds came in different lengths and with different types of chemical reactivity. In general, Pauling said, there were three different types of carbon-carbon bonds—single, double, and triple bonds. Some substances, however, had chemical properties and bond lengths that seemed to be in between these types. For example, benzene is a ring of six carbon atoms, each with one hydrogen atom.

Thinking about the nature of the chemical bond led Pauling to develop the concept of "resonance," which has to do with molecular structure. This states that the true structure of a molecule can be described by a sum of several simpler structures. The concept of resonance is a difficult one. It is drawn from both classical and quantum mechanics—which are complex parts of physics. In applying these ideas to chemical bonding, however, Pauling also drew heavily on his knowledge of laboratory observations in chemistry. Perhaps his greatest genius lay in his ability—unique at that time—to combine these two very different fields. Most quantum physicists hardly understood chemical bonding—and most chemists knew little of quantum physics.

Exploring the Chemical Bond

Throughout 1929, Pauling continued to apply his knowledge of quantum theory to chemical bonding. He had now been working on this subject for more than seven years. Pauling was making important contributions to scientists' understanding of the properties, or traits, of matter, which is the focus of chemistry. In 1930, Pauling returned to Europe and visited Germany to learn more about the latest thinking on quantum physics, resonance, valence, and hybrid bonds.

He put his expertise in quantum mechanics and chemistry to good use. In December 1930, Pauling figured out how to make some mathematical calculations of hybrid orbital bonds that had puzzled him for two years. Realizing that he was on the verge of a major discovery, Pauling completed the calculations. The results filled him with excitement.

Hybridized bonds, said Pauling, were able to resonate between what were called "covalent" and "ionic" forms of bonding. Chemists had defined a covalent bond as one in which two atoms shared a pair of electrons equally. Ionic bonds occurred when one atom had a strong enough "pull" to draw the pair of electrons toward itself, so that one atom would develop a negative charge and the other would develop a positive charge.

In 1931, Pauling published a paper entitled "The Nature of the Chemical Bond." The paper, which filled 34 pages in the April issue of *The Journal of the American Chemical Society*, detailed his six rules for chemical bonding. Pauling had further developed his earlier ideas about resonance. In the paper, he concluded that—under the laws of hybridization and resonance—atoms must bond in certain definite patterns. As a result, molecules would all have definite geometrical shapes, and these shapes could be predicted. And if the shapes and natures of the molecules could be predicted, then scientists might also be able to predict how a new substance would act, even before it was created.

Pauling's paper electrified the scientific world. By using what became known as "Pauling's rules," scientists hoped to be able to understand the structure of many molecules. On the basis of Pauling's work, for example, scientists were able to figure out and describe the structures of certain solid crystals. Some of these crystals had baffled them for decades.

Satisfied with his work on crystals, Pauling turned his attention to a different type of matter: gases. While in Germany in 1930, he had visited Austrian-born scientist Hermann Mark in order to learn about a technique called electron diffraction. Mark and his associates had found a way to shoot a beam of electrons through a jet of gas in a vacuum tube. Depending on the type of gas, the electrons would diffract, or scatter, in different patterns. These patterns were then recorded on photographic paper, as in X-ray diffraction. Electron diffraction took less than one second, however, allowing scientists to study substances that changed form rapidly. Thus, this method seemed superior to X-ray diffraction as a means of studying hydrogen and other simple substances that were not solid at room temperature. The technique also worked well with unstable, quickly changing substances. In the years that followed, Pauling and his assistants refined Mark's techniques, using them to analyze more than 200 substances.

An Honored Young Scientist

The year 1931 brought many honors and awards. Not yet 30 years old, Linus Pauling was already being recognized and hailed as a great scientist. The American Chemical Society called him the most promising young researcher in the United States. Pauling became the youngest person ever to be voted a member of the National Academy of Sciences.

Pauling's family was expanding as well. Another son, Peter Jeffress Pauling, was born in February 1931. Later that year, the Paulings spent several months in Cambridge, Massachusetts, where Linus had a temporary appointment at the Massachusetts Institute of Technology (MIT). And in May 1932, the family welcomed their first and only daughter, Linda Helen.

"The Nature of the Chemical Bond"

In 1931, the Pauling family included two young sons—
Linus, Jr. (standing), and Peter (in Ava Helen's arms).

New Horizons in Biology

During the 1930s, Pauling became fascinated with biological questions. These were thrilling years for biologists, especially those studying heredity, the process by which traits are passed from one generation to the next. Thomas Hunt Morgan won the Nobel Prize in Physiology or Medicine in 1933 for his work in this field. Morgan had come to Caltech in 1929. By studying millions of fruit flies and watching thousands of new generations, he had made important findings, leading to the new field of science called genetics.

Another person who greatly influenced Pauling during these years was Howard Lucas, who had come to Caltech from Ohio State University. Lucas was the first scientist to write a textbook on organic chemistry—the study of matter based on carbon and hydrogen, which includes nearly all of the chemicals in living organisms. This field had been regarded by most inorganic chemists—who study nonliving matter—as unscientific, even second-rate.

Pauling himself had once felt little enthusiasm about organic chemistry. Now, he found himself gravitating to the biology department, where Morgan, Alfred Sturtevant, and Calvin Bridges formed the core of a top-quality faculty. Pauling attended some of Morgan's lectures on genetics and was fascinated to learn about a phenomenon called "crossing-over." Morgan had concluded that, during cell division, the chromosomes, which contain genes, may get wrapped around each other or overlap. This may lead to breaking at the crossing point. Then, the broken sections may reconnect to a different chromosome. This can lead to mutations (changes) of traits that are then inherited.

Early Research into Proteins

During this time, Linus Pauling had another one of his flashes of insight, while studying a piece of asbestos under the microscope. As he pulled the material apart, he noticed that the fibers were as thin as a strand of hair. Pauling commented to an assistant that, since they could study these kinds of fibers, perhaps they could also investigate living, or organic, fibers such as those that compose hair, muscles, and fingernails.

Protein, a substance that would occupy Pauling's attention for several years, is an essential part of living cells. Protein is needed for cell growth and repair. In deciding to figure out the structure of protein, Pauling had not chosen an easy task. Inorganic crystals are small and simple in comparison to protein molecules, which are large and complex. Pauling began his new course of study with the protein molecules that compose hair.

Until 1935, he also continued to work regularly on chemical bonds. By the mid-1930s, Pauling was convinced that he had solved most of the basic problems related to understanding the chemical bond.

As he investigated proteins and chemical bonds, Pauling was asking important, basic questions about the structure and function of living cells. He viewed these questions from a "multidisciplinary" perspective—applying ideas from biology, chemistry, and physics. At the time, this was a fairly new approach.

It seemed likely to him that the shape of certain cells in the body would determine their function. For example, certain blood cells fight disease, while others carry oxygen. The

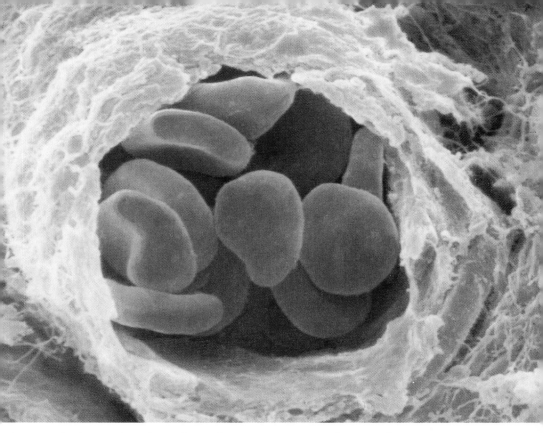

A photo taken through an electron microscope shows red blood cells moving through a small artery. (This photography process produces colors that are not true to life.)

atoms and molecules of these cells must be joined in such a way that they are able to do these tasks, he concluded.

The years 1934 and 1935 found Linus Pauling hard at work on studies of blood. Pauling designed experiments in which he explored the magnetic properties of hemoglobin, a large protein molecule that carries oxygen to the cells of the body. He found that hemoglobin in arterial blood (blood being carried away from the heart in arteries) was repelled by a magnet, yet it was attracted to a magnet when found in venous blood (blood traveling toward the heart in veins). Through a series of experiments, he and a graduate student, Charles Coryell, discovered some key features of this vital

"The Nature of the Chemical Bond"

molecule. For example, they found that iron atoms, located at the center of hemoglobin molecules, bind with oxygen from the air that is inhaled into the lungs.

EXPANDING ROLES

In 1935, Arthur Noyes died. Now, Pauling was asked to assume Noyes's post as chairman of Caltech's department of chemistry and its two chemistry laboratories, while reducing his teaching functions.

As department chairman, Pauling was known for passing on to others many administrative duties. He didn't like those tasks that took precious time away from his research. By now, his mind was occupied with three different subjects: the structure of the protein molecule, molecular bonds, and the structure and functioning of hemoglobin. He continued to write scientific papers. By age 30, he had already published 50 research papers.

At home, Ava Helen and Linus welcomed their fourth child, Edward Crellin Pauling, in June 1937. He would become known as "Crellin" in honor of one of the financial supporters of Caltech, for whom Crellin Laboratory had been named.

Now six in number, the Pauling family needed more room. Linus and Ava Helen decided to build a home, using their own design, on a wooded lot a few miles from Caltech. The rambling house took the shape of a molecule, and it had plenty of room for Linus's book-filled study, a children's playroom, and Ava Helen's piano. Students and faculty from Caltech enjoyed the lively, informal parties that the Paulings liked to host at their new home.

DECODING GIANT MOLECULES

In 1937, Pauling gave a series of lectures on chemical bonding at Cornell University in Ithaca, New York. While at Cornell, Pauling met the famous Austrian-American biochemist Karl Landsteiner, who was then 69 years old. Landsteiner had won the 1930 Nobel Prize in Physiology or Medicine for his work in classifying the four major blood groups—A, B, AB, and O. He had also done important work in immunology (the study of the body's disease-fighting system). In 1908, Landsteiner had isolated the virus that causes the crippling disease polio. (A virus is a particle—smaller than a cell and composed solely of DNA and protein—that can gain entry to a cell of a host and take over its reproductive machinery.) After hearing Pauling deliver a lecture on hemoglobin, Landsteiner invited him to visit his laboratory, where they discussed blood chemistry and various experiments.

Chemical bonds in living molecules posed new and different problems from those Pauling had studied before. Of particular interest were the strength and weakness of hydrogen bonds. (Hydrogen bonds are the weak but important interactions between a hydrogen atom in one molecule and an oxygen or nitrogen atom in another.) Some European scientists had been trying to decipher proteins by using X-ray crystallography. In 1934, British scientist Desmond Bernal had shown that these giant molecules could be studied in the form of crystals. Bernal's work supported the theory that the molecules took an orderly shape, rather than a chaotic or random form. The amino acids—the subunits of proteins—must be organized in a geometric pattern, rather than in a loose, haphazard way, thought Pauling and his associates.

The Alphabet of Life

Proteins make up all body tissues as well as composing enzymes and some hormones. Scientists had puzzled over the structure and function of proteins long before Linus Pauling studied them. In 1900, a German chemist named Emil Hermann Fischer determined that proteins are made up of amino acids, which, in turn, are made up of carbon, oxygen, hydrogen, nitrogen, and small amounts of other elements. Fischer, awarded the Nobel Prize for Chemistry in 1902, had previously spent years discovering the atomic makeup of several sugars, which he then synthesized in his lab.

The 24 amino acids found in protein molecules have been referred to as the "alphabet of life." These acids unite to form peptides, structures that combine to form still larger groups called polypeptides (*poly* means many). Polypeptides are long strings of amino acids that, under normal conditions, are found coiled in a variety of different three-dimensional shapes called "tertiary structures."

By the 1930s, scientists believed that the traits of a protein depended on its chemical composition—the types, amounts, and proportions of amino acids. But they had not figured out the pattern of the acids. Some protein molecules contain hundreds of amino acids and hundreds of thousands of atoms. Scientists could not decipher the structure of such complicated molecules using only mathematical calculations.

Early in his studies of proteins, Pauling decided that all of these large molecules were polypeptides. Because the primary structure of the molecules took a chain form, he thought that they must be held together in their tertiary structure with some kind of specific chemical links—the hydrogen bonds that he had been studying for more than 15 years and had written so much about. Being weaker than other covalent chemical bonds, hydrogen bonds are more easily broken, especially when exposed to heat. Such conditions cause the molecules to fall apart, changing their orderly configuration. Pauling cited, as an example, the way that egg white changes when it is cooked.

Polypeptide chain of amino acids

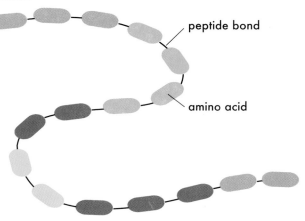

peptide bond

amino acid

Three-dimensional protein molecule

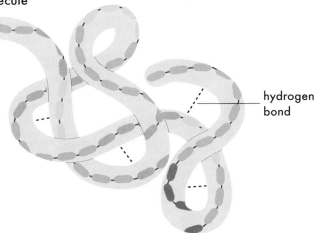

hydrogen bond

Pauling made many discoveries about protein structure: both the primary, or polypeptide-chain, structure and the more complex three-dimensional structure.

Back at Caltech, Pauling teamed up with Robert Corey, a leader in protein chemistry. They wanted to figure out the structure of protein molecules. The two began by studying polypeptide chains—the chains of amino acids that make up protein molecules.

As they studied proteins, Pauling, Corey, and other researchers were burdened by some inaccurate data. W. T. Astbury, a prominent British crystallographer, had taken X-ray photos of protein molecules and had drawn incorrect conclusions from them. Astbury had presented his work and conclusions at a symposium in Cold Spring Harbor, New York, in 1938. As Pauling developed various three-dimensional chain models for proteins, he tried hard to make them fit Astbury's data. It occurred to him that Astbury may have erred in his conclusions, but Pauling was not sure what the correct answers should be. It would be much later—in 1950—that other scientists would realize that Astbury had interpreted some data incorrectly.

In the meantime, Linus Pauling and Robert Corey came up with a plan to help them reach their goal of deciphering the patterns of amino acids that make up proteins. They would start by figuring out the exact nature of the structures in the main amino acids in proteins, hoping that this would yield information about the chains and the larger protein structure.

They began by looking at chains with only two amino acids. As they deciphered these small chains, the findings agreed with their early theory that protein chains were "planar" in structure—that is, they did not rotate freely, turning and twisting in an indefinite number of directions. Proving that peptide bonds were planar would be a major step in solving the molecular structure of proteins.

COMPETING THEORIES

While Pauling was working on the nature of peptide bonds, so were other distinguished scientists. Among them was Dorothy Wrinch, a faculty member at Oxford University in England, who had published a number of acclaimed scientific papers and highly regarded books. She thought that amino acids in proteins might connect with each other in more complex ways than end-to-end. Her theory about proteins, called the "cyclol hypothesis," differed from Pauling's. As researchers analyzed the opposing viewpoints, they sided with one scientist or the other. Some wrote to Pauling suggesting that Wrinch might be right.

In January 1938, Pauling and Wrinch met to discuss their work. The meeting was not friendly, and Wrinch avoided Pauling from then on. Both scientists had strong personalities. Wrinch had been called a demanding, assertive, even abrasive person. Linus Pauling could be critical, intimidating, and difficult to talk to in certain situations.

Various historians have pointed out that, during those years, women scientists often had to fight for acceptance in a male-dominated profession. But it is very unlikely that Pauling rejected Wrinch's theory simply because she was a woman. Rather, it is more likely that he rejected it because he believed that the cyclol structure was too unstable to be the correct explanation for the structure of protein molecules. Besides, Pauling had urged administrators of Caltech to admit women graduate students, something they finally did when he headed the chemistry department there. And throughout his life, Pauling always showed great respect for his wife's judgment and ideas. Linus Pauling was a man who always enjoyed the company of intelligent people, both men and women.

Pauling's textbook *The Nature of the Chemical Bond* was published in 1939. It has since been hailed as one of the most influential science textbooks ever written. Pauling dedicated the book to Gilbert N. Lewis, whose work had inspired him to study chemical bonds years before and who was now also his friend. The book was used as a textbook for many years in different countries. Readers praised Pauling's writing and said that he made the subject understandable even for people who were not scientific experts. Yet not everyone accepted all his theories. Some chemists said that he had based his theories on certain unproven ideas about molecular structures.

ILLNESS AND RECOVERY

Pauling remained confident about his work, which was interrupted by illness in the fall of 1940. He had begun feeling very tired, and his complexion, usually rosy, looked pale. At first, he blamed his demanding work schedule for these symptoms, but as time went on, his family urged him to see a doctor. Pauling was diagnosed with glomerulo nephritis, or Bright's disease, a serious inflammation of the kidneys that was sometimes fatal in those days. His doctor advised bed rest and medication. He also put Pauling on a strict diet featuring foods that were without salt and low in protein.

During this time, Pauling was fascinated to learn about nutritional approaches to healing. This was something his physician, Dr. Thomas Addis, promoted. Addis also gave Pauling vitamin supplements, including vitamin C, a substance Pauling would one day explore with tremendous interest. For several years, Pauling remained under Addis's care for recurring nephritis. He later credited the doctor with saving his life.

By 1941, Pauling was feeling better. That year, he was honored with the Nichols Medal. In bestowing this award, the New York Section of the American Chemical Society recognized Pauling's "distinguished and pioneering work on the application of quantum mechanics to chemistry and on the size and shape of molecules." It noted the amazing body of his work. At that time, Pauling was barely 40 years old.

He received an offer that autumn to head the research department at Shell Oil Company, a position that provided him a much higher salary, more research facilities, and a larger staff than he had at Caltech. Caltech was willing to increase his salary, although not nearly to the amount offered by Shell. Caltech also offered him additional research space and the chance to do more medical research. Pauling chose to stay at Caltech. He enjoyed the academic atmosphere, which was something he would not have had at a large corporation. Working in industry, he would also have been less independent. Pauling was used to publishing his findings, and that, too, would change in the more secretive, profit-oriented atmosphere of a corporation.

Pauling continued to work on the structure of proteins. Some pieces of this puzzle were gradually coming together. But as 1941 drew to a close, dramatic historical events would drive his work in new directions.

A
TUMULTUOUS
DECADE

Like other Americans, Linus Pauling had been deeply concerned about the war that had been expanding steadily in Europe. In 1933, Adolf Hitler's Nazi Party had risen to power in Germany. Hitler had vowed to solve Germany's economic woes and restore the country's national pride, which was severely damaged after the nation was defeated in World War I. After disbanding the labor unions and taking control of the press and other institutions in order to stifle dissent (opposition or protest), Hitler launched radical policies of racial and ethnic intolerance.

In 1938, Germany annexed Austria. During the next two years, Nazi troops invaded, then occupied, Poland,

Czechoslovakia, Holland, Belgium, and France. The Nazis began persecuting Jews and others whom they considered "inferior" to their ideal of a master German race. As the situation worsened and all Jews were banned from teaching at universities, many scientists and other citizens fled Germany—and Europe—if they could. Among them was Jewish physicist Albert Einstein, who went first to Belgium, then to the United States.

The Allies—England, France, and Russia—fought against the Axis powers of Italy, Germany, and Japan. Then, on December 7, 1941, the United States actively joined World War II on the side of the Allies. That morning, Japanese bombers had launched a deadly surprise attack on the U.S. naval base at Pearl Harbor, Hawaii.

CONCERNS ABOUT SOCIAL PROBLEMS

The war deepened Linus Pauling's interest in politics. He had first become politically active during the Great Depression in the 1930s. Pauling had supported President Franklin D. Roosevelt's reelection in 1936, believing that the Democratic President's New Deal policies were the best answer for the widespread poverty and unemployment that plagued America during the Depression. This was a turnabout, since Pauling had been a registered Republican who voted for Herbert Hoover. Ava Helen, however, had long supported liberal political candidates and social reform, having grown up in a family that was especially concerned about the poor and oppressed.

Pauling despised the Axis actions in Europe and volunteered to aid the American war effort. Many of his students

Standing Up for Their Beliefs

During the early 1940s, the Paulings' gardener was a young man of Japanese-American descent. After the United States entered World War II, there was intense hostility toward the Japanese. The U.S. government set up internment camps for Japanese Americans. These citizens were forcibly detained in the camps, where it was believed they would be safe from crimes against them. Internment also satisfied suspicious people who thought some of these American citizens might actually be spies for the enemy Japan.

Some Americans opposed these camps, arguing that they violated these citizens' civil liberties. They believed that law enforcement officials should try harder to ensure the safety of Japanese Americans in their homes and communities. In recent years, the U.S. government formally apologized to the victims of internment policies and gave them some compensation for their lost property.

Ava Helen and Linus Pauling refused to fire their gardener, feeling that it was unjust. It was the first of many times that they would uphold their principles regardless of what it cost them personally. They began receiving hate mail and anonymous threatening letters and telephone calls. Someone painted their garage door with a red Japanese flag and wrote: "Americans die but we love Japs [a negative term for Japanese]." After Pauling notified the police, a guard was assigned to watch their home 24 hours a day, but the police did not actively pursue those who performed this act of vandalism.

Although frightened, the Paulings stood firm. The gardener kept his job until he left to serve in the U.S. Army. By this time, Ava Helen was actively opposing internment through her work with the American Civil Liberties Union (ACLU), for which she served as a board member in Los Angeles, California. Earlier, she had helped to found the Southern California ACLU. She remained committed to peace, civil liberties, and human rights throughout her life and delivered many lectures on peace in the United States and 40 other countries. In 1981, the ACLU honored Ava Helen Pauling with a special ceremony, praising her lifelong "concern for justice and freedom" in the face of opposition and harassment.

served in the armed forces, and Linus, Jr., just 17 years old at the time, enlisted in the U.S. Air Corps. The Paulings, thus, became one of many American families who had to worry about loved ones fighting overseas. Ava Helen went to work in the Caltech laboratory, since the lab was short of personnel during the war.

During the war years, there was pressure on Caltech and other research facilities to work on scientific problems that would help the military effort. Pauling developed rocket fuels, gunpowder formulas, and liquid propellants. He also designed an instrument to measure the oxygen pressure in submarines. The meter that he developed was later adapted for use in hospitals as well.

Pauling continued to conduct more biological studies. In 1942, he became interested in blood proteins called "antibodies" that the body creates to defend itself against disease organisms. When viruses and bacteria invade the body, antibodies work to destroy or disable them. Pauling's work in this area had actually begun in 1939 when his interest in molecular medicine led him to think more intensely about antigens–antibody reactions. Antigens, such as those found in bacteria or viruses, are chemical materials against which antibodies react.

At this time, scientists theorized that certain forces existed between antibodies and antigens, causing them to come together and enabling the antibodies to neutralize or destroy the dangerous antigens. Scientists wondered how this could happen, however, because the bonds between the molecules were weak and would not hold the molecules together in such a way that this reaction could occur.

Pauling thought that a theory called "complementariness," which had been applied in other chemical situations,

Interlocking Proteins

Molecular shape is very important in antigen–antibody bonding. The two molecules must fit together exactly—like a lock and key.

offered what scientists might refer to as "an elegant solution." The shapes of the molecules might fit together in a complementary way by interlocking—fitting together like a lock and key. The surfaces of the antibody and antigen molecules would be close at all points. That way, the weak forces would be pulling the molecules together all over, rather than at just a couple of points, with equal force. This helped to show how antibodies are specific to the antigens they are designed to fight.

Pauling's group showed how the production of antibodies in the blood is spurred by changes in the shapes of special protein molecules called "serum globulins." During one series of scientific experiments, they demonstrated this process, producing antibodies in a test tube by altering the shape of serum globulins.

With Don Campbell, Pauling also headed a team that developed a synthetic blood plasma that was cheaper and easier to obtain than natural blood plasma. Plasma is the liquid part of blood that does not contain the red or white cells. Large amounts of plasma were needed during the war for transfusions, to replace blood lost by wounded soldiers. The synthetic plasma had a gelatin base and was called "oxypolygelatin."

The Manhattan Project

While Pauling and others conducted biological research, a group of scientists from America and war-torn Europe were involved in top-secret work in Los Alamos, New Mexico. The now-famous Manhattan Project, as the enterprise was called, required the scientists to work almost around the clock to design and build atomic bombs for the Allied war effort. The director, physicist Robert Oppenheimer, had assembled one of the most brilliant groups of scientists who ever participated in a joint undertaking.

Oppenheimer and Pauling were friends as well as fellow scientists. Knowing about Pauling's interest in minerals, Oppenheimer had given him some unusual specimens over the years. While putting together the team at Los Alamos, Oppenheimer had asked Pauling to direct the chemistry section, but Pauling declined. He never explained in public why he had not taken part in the project. Biographer Anthony Serafini and other interviewers have speculated that Pauling had concerns about the making and potential use of atomic weapons and so stayed out of the project. Others, however, believe that Pauling simply felt that he could be more useful where he was.

Even before World War II ended, some scientists began to worry about the atomic bomb and its potential for disaster. In 1944, a group of concerned people formed the Scientists Movement. It was led by Hungarian-born scientist Leo Szilard, who was then at the University of Chicago. Szilard had been one of the first people to recognize that atomic bombs were a possibility and that the Nazis might build them first. He had urged the U.S. government to work on atomic weapons and had been one of the chief scientists on the team that developed the first nuclear chain reaction—produced by nuclear fission (splitting of atoms), which causes great energy to be released.

The Scientists Movement included another colleague of Pauling's, physicist Arthur H. Compton, who believed that nations needed an international administration to police and control nuclear weaponry. Other Manhattan Project

Victims of the bombing of Hiroshima in 1945 wait for medical assistance after an atomic bomb demolished the city.

scientists, including Oppenheimer himself, would eventually join in this effort.

In the meantime, the work of the Manhattan Project went on. The group successfully developed two kinds of atomic bombs, one made with uranium, the other with plutonium. Germany surrendered in May 1945, but Japan continued to fight. Japanese military leaders vowed never to surrender. After listening to various advisers, President Harry S. Truman authorized the use of atomic bombs against Japan.

The first bomb was dropped on the city of Hiroshima, Japan, on August 6, 1945. The power of the bomb was estimated to be as great as 20 million tons of TNT, an explosive. Of the 300,000 people who lived in Hiroshima, more than 100,000 may have died that day. Others died in the days that followed, from severe burns or radiation sickness caused by the atomic blast. Survivors endured terrible burn scars and other injuries. Many later developed cancer and other diseases at rates much higher than normal. Eyewitnesses would later call the scene catastrophic, a "hell on earth." Like others, Linus Pauling saw the newspaper headlines that day—ATOMIC BOMB DROPPED ON JAPAN—and read about this unprecedented weapon.

Three days later, Japan had still not surrendered, and a second bomb was dropped, this time on the city of Nagasaki. Again, there were tens of thousands of deaths and injuries and vast destruction. On August 10, Japan agreed to surrender, ending World War II.

CONCERNS ABOUT ATOMIC WEAPONS

The bombings ignited mixed feelings around the world and an ethical and moral controversy that continues to this day. Pauling was gravely concerned about the implications of atomic weapons and about America's responsibility for having unleashed them.

For her part, Ava Helen became even more committed to the cause of world peace. She told Linus that no other human achievement would mean anything if the world were destroyed. She said that they must both work to end war. Ava Helen increased her involvement with the Women's International League for Peace and Freedom (WILPF), a group that was started by the pacifist (someone who opposes war) and reformer Jane Addams. In 1889, Addams had founded Hull House, a social-work settlement in a poverty-stricken section of Chicago. Pauling delivered lectures in which he strongly opposed nuclear weapons, saying that they had made war obsolete. He studied international relations and politics so that he could speak more knowledgeably on the subjects.

In 1945, Vannevar Bush, a government official, asked Pauling to join a committee authorized by President Truman to study the future of medical research in America. Pauling accepted at once. Some critics said that he was chiefly interested in the power and prestige of this committee, but he disagreed. The committee was involved with two of his most deeply held interests: medicine and research.

It was true that World War II had made "big science" a reality, merging politics and science as never before. The Manhattan Project had cost $2 billion. And, after the war, a great deal of federal money was being channeled into various scientific pursuits.

The Postwar Years

By 1946, with the war over, scientific centers tried to resume their normal operation. A recurrence of Bright's disease left Pauling feeling poorly, but despite this, he traveled to several major scientific meetings. While visiting colleagues at universities around the country, he sometimes took time to speak with graduate students about his work. As a professor, one of his roles was to find excellent students who could come to Caltech. He also tried to help his own graduate students pursue further studies in the right settings.

At home, meanwhile, Linus, Jr., had returned from the U.S. Air Corps. He was in college, planning to enter medical school, after which he would study psychiatry. Peter planned to study biology and chemistry after he finished high school the next year. Later, he received his doctoral degree, completing his studies at the Cavendish Laboratory, where James Watson and Francis Crick would soon discover the secrets of DNA in 1953. Linda enjoyed the arts—music, dancing, and painting. She later graduated from Reed College in Portland, Oregon. At times, Linda also worked as a nanny/housekeeper for the Crick family. In 1957, she married Barclay Kamb, a geology professor at Caltech. Crellin, age nine in 1946, would later study biochemistry and genetics.

The year 1946 brought more changes at Caltech. Pauling's friend and former adviser Roscoe Dickinson died of colon cancer. This was a big personal loss for Pauling. Max Delbruck came to the institute around this time. Delbruck, a famous German-American quantum physicist and biologist, had been studying genetics. He specialized in the study of bacteriophages. These are viruses that attack bacteria and are the simplest forms of all viruses. Pauling enjoyed discussing science with the versatile Delbruck.

In 1946, Pauling completed a new textbook, *General Chemistry*. Like his first text, this one would become a standard in college chemistry courses for decades. He was also elected president of the American Chemical Society.

The Paulings went to the White House in 1948 to attend a ceremony at which Linus Pauling received the Presidential Medal of Merit from President Truman. In giving the award, Truman recognized Pauling's contributions to science and humanity and praised his wartime service.

The Alpha-Helix

Back in the laboratory, Pauling and Robert Corey had completed a substantial amount of work on amino acids. At that point, Pauling was able to narrow down the number of configurations that the protein molecule might take. It had been 11 years since he had conceived his theory about how protein chains are put together, and the research had confirmed his initial ideas. His theories about the dimensions of the molecule seemed to work, too. Now, he felt ready to figure out what he called "the problem of coiling the polypeptide chain." He was ready to move on from the primary protein structure to the more complex three-dimensional one.

In the fall of 1947, Pauling traveled to Oxford University, near London, England, as a visiting professor. Ava Helen accompanied him and spent much time attending lectures at Oxford. Their children Peter (then age 16), Linda (15), and Crellin (10) also went along. They attended school in England during that time.

The next spring, a flare-up of nephritis, along with a cold, confined Pauling to bed, where he passed the time reading detective novels and westerns. While bedridden, Pauling's mind wandered to keratin, the protein whose structure he had recently been trying to decipher. He sketched the keratin molecule, with its atoms and chemical bonds, on paper, then began twisting the paper in different ways. As he folded, a helical, or spiral, model began to emerge—one that seemed to fit the data that had been gathered through X-ray diffraction. Within a few hours of experimenting with folding, he had discovered the alpha-helix.

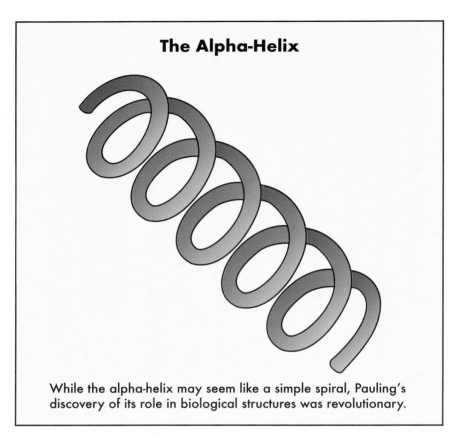

The Alpha-Helix

While the alpha-helix may seem like a simple spiral, Pauling's discovery of its role in biological structures was revolutionary.

Pauling had made one of his greatest discoveries that day in 1948. The alpha-helix would have a profound influence on the way scientists thought about biological tissues. It provided a model of how biological polymers (long chains of repeating structural units, such as the peptide chain of a protein) can form specific, ordered, three-dimensional structures. This allowed them to envision that normal cells might differ from those of diseased individuals due to differences in protein structure. Once these chemical abnormalities were understood, new drugs might be designed to bring cures. But Pauling did not publish his alpha-helix structure yet. He wanted to resolve certain aspects of the theory first.

Back in Pasadena, Pauling and Corey delved into a variety of other protein tissues, such as fingernail, hair, and muscle. They concluded that the helix was the basic shape for proteins in humans and other animals and that their conclusions fit the latest findings about proteins (later findings would modify this conclusion).

In November 1950, Pauling and Corey published a brief notice about their findings in *The Journal of the American*

Pauling was famous for his colorful visual models of chemical structures.

Chemical Society. In April and May the next year, they published detailed articles about the atomic structures of numerous proteins, exciting the interest of biologists and chemists throughout the world. Among those scientists was biologist James Dewey Watson, then a graduate student in Denmark, whose goal was to figure out the structure of DNA. He would later do just that, working it out with British physicist Francis Crick. Watson later recalled that, after reading about the alpha-helix, he knew that he must study X-ray crystallography in order to study molecular structure. He made arrangements to do so at the Cavendish Laboratory in Cambridge, England.

As was his habit, Professor Pauling helped his students at Caltech to understand the alpha-helix theory by showing them a necklacelike chain of colorful plastic bubbles. When he delivered his lectures on the alpha-helix, the hall was crowded with not only his students but also scientists and other professors.

Studying Sickle-Cell Anemia

These new insights into protein molecules led Pauling back to an earlier interest: the study of how hemoglobin takes up oxygen in the bloodstream. In 1945, Pauling had attended a dinner in New York City where physicians discussed sickle-cell anemia, a disease in which red blood cells are deformed. They told Pauling about the suffering that comes from this disease. Patients are prone to blood clots, painful clogging of red blood cells in the spleen, infections, and fatigue due to oxygen deprivation. About 50 percent of people with the disease die before age 30.

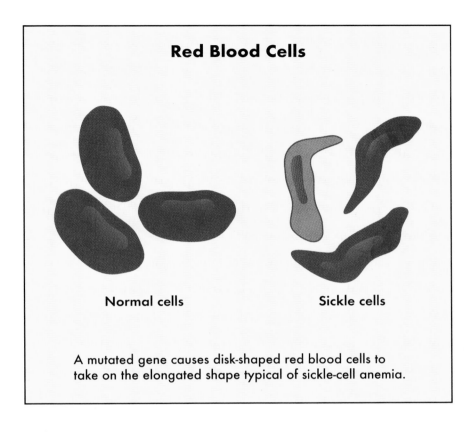

Red Blood Cells

Normal cells   Sickle cells

A mutated gene causes disk-shaped red blood cells to take on the elongated shape typical of sickle-cell anemia.

The disease is found most often in people of African descent. About 10 percent of all African Americans have a recessive gene for the sickle-cell trait, which means that they do not have the disease itself but can pass the trait on to their children. One in every 500 African-American children is born with two recessive sickle-cell genes, meaning that he or she will have the disease. A small percentage of people of Mediterranean and Indian descent also carry the gene.

As Pauling considered sickle-cell anemia, the thought occurred to him that this might well be a disease of the hemoglobin molecule caused by a mutated gene. Normally, red blood cells are shaped like disks, enabling them to move smoothly through the blood vessels. In people with sickle-cell disease, the cells have this normal disk shape in arterial blood. But when in venous blood, traveling back toward the heart through veins, the cells assume an elongated crescent shape resembling a sickle. These misshapen red blood cells are rigid, and they tend to clump, so they do not pass smoothly, at the normal speed, through blood vessels.

Through his work with geneticist and Nobel Laureate George Beadle, Pauling knew something about mutations of genes and their role in causing disease, which were Beadle's specialties. Pauling set out to test his theory that normal, healthy hemoglobin differs from that found in people with sickle-cell disease.

First, the research team separated sickled cells from normal cells, a difficult task. Swedish scientists had tried a process known as "electrophoresis," and other scientists had refined the technique in 1949. Using electrophoresis, Pauling's team confirmed that sickle-cell hemoglobin had different electromagnetic properties from those of normal hemoglobin. When different samples of hemoglobin were exposed to an electric field, the sickle protein moved more slowly across the field than normal hemoglobin did.

The team then examined blood hemoglobin from people who had inherited one sickle-cell gene and one normal gene. They found that these people had both kinds of hemoglobin in the blood: some moved slowly, while the rest moved at a normal speed. But there was enough normal hemoglobin to prevent severe anemia and symptoms.

Later, in 1956, the mutation of the gene responsible for sickle-cell disease was found by German-American chemist Vernon Ingram. He determined that, in sickle-cell anemia, something went wrong during the process of making the protein chain of hemoglobin. One of the 574 amino acids in hemoglobin was different in sickle-cell hemoglobin. On the part of the chain where the amino acid valine belonged, there was instead a molecule of glutamic acid. Chemically, this made the sickle hemoglobin less acidic than normal, causing it to move more slowly.

Once again, Pauling had conducted groundbreaking research. His findings, which were published in the November 25, 1949, issue of *Science* magazine under the title "Sickle-Cell Anemia: A Molecular Disease," launched many discussions and paved the way for other important research. Now nearly 50 years old, Pauling's urge to understand blood chemistry had led to a new way of looking at disease. Most important, it proved that diseases could be caused by a molecular disorder. His work on sickle-cell disease strengthened the science of genetics and paved the way for gene-therapy techniques that would come several decades later.

Science
and
Politics

During these years of discovery, Linus Pauling juggled his scientific work with political activism. He gave numerous lectures about the dangers of nuclear weapons and was among those who advocated a ban on nuclear testing. He also thought that the United States should not go forward with work on the hydrogen bomb (a more destructive weapon than the earlier uranium and plutonium atomic bombs). The H-bomb, as it was known, was developed based on the work of physicists Edward Teller, Stanislaw Ulam, and others.

While working with groups that promoted world peace, Pauling became friends with another giant of twentieth-century science, physicist Albert Einstein. Einstein had often discussed his philosophy of life and his views on ethics and world issues. The two men met in California on January 12, 1950, a meeting that left Pauling feeling optimistic about the potential for nuclear-weapons disarmament. He also kept in touch with Leo Szilard regularly.

UNDER ATTACK

It was not surprising that Pauling's speeches against nuclear weapons and his pacifist activities brought him to the attention of various government officials who had decided to investigate any citizens or organizations suspected of Communist or leftist sympathies. In the fall of 1950, Pauling was handed a subpoena—a legal summons—that required him to meet with the California State Senate Investigating Committee on Education.

Pauling objected to the idea of requiring federal- and state-government employees to take special "loyalty oaths," as was then being required throughout America. He also firmly believed that no citizen should be required to declare his or her political affiliations at hearings conducted by government committees investigating communism. He said that the idea of forcing citizens to publicly declare their political beliefs went against Americans' constitutional right to freedom of expression. Outspoken as usual, Pauling told the California committee that he regarded its questions as improper.

As a result, Pauling was called back to the committee for more questioning, and the committee threatened to cite him for contempt. He continued to object and refused to answer questions asked by the committee that he felt was

McCarthyism

The postwar years saw an arms race escalating between the United States and the Soviet Union, which was controlled by a Communist regime. The Cold War years, as they were called, sparked suspicious attitudes, even paranoia, toward communism and those who either belonged to the Communist Party or failed to denounce it.

Senator Joseph R. McCarthy of Wisconsin organized a special congressional committee to investigate charges of communism. He launched this effort in February 1950, when he charged that the U.S. State Department had been infiltrated (penetrated secretly) by Communists. The charge was not proven. Nonetheless, as chairman of the Senate Permanent Investigating Subcommittee, McCarthy set out to identify any Americans who might have this political affiliation, especially those working in government. McCarthy accused them of being disloyal to the United States (even though the Communist Party was legal).

The House Un-American Activities Committee went after citizens from all walks of life, many of them in the film and television industry, the arts, and sciences. McCarthyism—as this anti-Communist crusade became known—gathered steam, and was especially intense in California, where many members of the film industry were targeted for investigation. (The Communist Party had been active in that state during the Depression of the 1930s.)

Those brought before the committee for questioning were asked not only to discuss their own activities and politics but to reveal the

unconstitutional by its very nature. Outside the building where the hearings were being held, he spoke to the press and declared that he had never been and was not then a Communist. He said that he was a "Rooseveltian Democrat" and stated that every citizen should become politically involved to protect the integrity of the nation.

names of any others whom they suspected of having Communist ties. Those who refused were threatened with possible jail terms. During the early 1950s, numerous people accused of "disloyalty" were "blacklisted"—denied employment in their fields. McCarthyism and related activities were eventually criticized, and Senator McCarthy was censured by the Senate in 1954 for his methods of intimidation. People would later call this series of hearings a "witch-hunt" that ruined the lives of many Americans.

Senator Joseph McCarthy (left) and Chief Committee Counsel Roy Cohn prepare to hold the final day of hearings in June 1954.

When the committee later asked him if he had made that comment to reporters, Pauling said yes. The committee then asked him directly if he was a Communist. Pauling refused to answer on the grounds that the question was improper.

Because Pauling was a prominent scientist, there was much publicity over his appearances before the committee.

While some of Pauling's colleagues agreed with him, or at least thought that he had a right to express controversial opinions, others were harshly critical. Some said that a scientist should stick to science and not become involved in politics. Others believed that Pauling should not speak out so forcefully because, they said, his personal opinions reflected on Caltech.

The trustees of Caltech discussed whether Pauling should be asked to resign as a professor. A committee of his colleagues, led by physics department chairman Robert Bacher, supported him, believing his worth as a scientist was more important than any doubts about his politics. Pauling was not asked to leave.

DEFENDING THE ALPHA-HELIX

At this time, Pauling was facing challenges on another front as well. Despite the evidence that he and Robert Corey had gathered to support the alpha-helix theory, not all scientists agreed with them. Some major researchers, including Max Perutz, William Lawrence Bragg, and other British biologists, had expressed doubts. These scientists believed that the structure of proteins would more likely take a simpler and more symmetrical pattern.

Pauling continued to defend his theory, but in 1952, he faced a formidable obstacle. An important scientific meeting was scheduled to take place in London, England, in April. Pauling had been asked to attend and deliver a paper defending the alpha-helix. W. T. Astbury, the organizer of the conference, had told Pauling that his appearance would be critical in gaining acceptance for the theory.

Preparing for the trip, Pauling applied for a passport, which citizens need in order to leave and reenter the country legally. But in February, the government passport office informed him that he would not be granted a passport. It cited the McCarran Act, which had been passed to prevent the exchange of secret information between Americans and spies in foreign lands.

It is not clear what dangerous "secrets" Pauling could have shared with any Communist agents. He was not involved in any scientific work, such as developing weapons or spacecraft, that touched on national security. His work in biology and chemistry was public, since he and other scientists discussed their work in journals and at universities and conferences. Besides, his theory about protein structure had been denounced by the Soviet Union, a Communist country. The Soviets opposed quantum mechanics and other theories that they believed contradicted their Marxist views. Marxism sees the world as predictable—known as a deterministic point of view. Quantum mechanics, on the other hand, embraces the idea of some indeterminism in the universe. For this reason, the Soviets had also rejected Pauling's theory of resonance.

Passport Controversy

The day that he received the startling news that his passport application had been denied, Pauling wrote directly to President Dwight D. Eisenhower, asking him to correct the matter. Calling himself "a loyal citizen of the United States," Pauling pointed out that he had never committed an unpatriotic or criminal act.

Instead of receiving a passport or reply directly from Eisenhower, Pauling received a letter simply saying that a member of the President's staff would investigate the matter. And even after Pauling sent the State Department a statement made under oath affirming that he was not a Communist, he was still denied a passport.

Shocked and outraged, Pauling told the British scientists that he could not attend the meeting. They expressed surprise and regret about the situation, as did many Americans. Pauling wrote to Albert Einstein, who personally wrote to Secretary of State Dean Acheson, defending Pauling's character and scientific genius. Einstein said that America's reputation would be hurt around the world if Pauling was denied the right to travel.

In spring 1952, a protest letter signed by many of the most famous scientists in America, including those who had worked to build the atomic bomb, was sent to Acheson and published in newspapers. A passport was still not issued, and Pauling missed the April meeting in London. Later on, he was given some short-term passports that he could use to attend single conferences but was not issued a regular passport.

As a result of this situation, Pauling was not able to explain his alpha-helix theory in person for a number of months. In addition, he was prevented from visiting London in 1952—a time when new and exciting research was being done on the DNA molecule. DNA, found in the cell nucleus, contains the information that enables genetic traits to be passed on from one generation to the next. Researchers at King's College in London possessed some key X-ray crystallography photographs of DNA. Working with Maurice Wilkins, Rosalind Franklin had produced more detailed photos than had ever been taken before. The photos helped

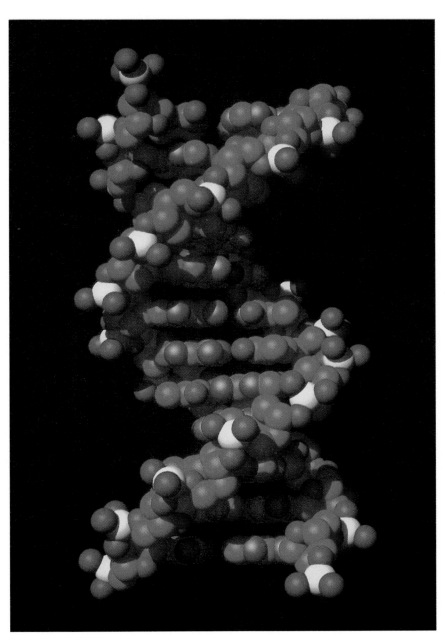

James Watson and Francis Crick discovered that the DNA molecule
has the structure of a double helix (shown here in a computer model).

A Rich Store of Ideas

By age 40, Linus Pauling was considered to be the foremost theoretical chemist in America, if not in the world. He was especially admired for his rich store of ideas and for his willingness to explore his intuitions even if supporting scientific data were not yet present.

In testing his various ideas, Pauling used the stochastic method—from a Greek word meaning "to divine the truth by conjecture." While investigating a new molecule, for example, he would learn everything he could about the physical properties and the X-ray data—whatever was available. Then, he would make educated guesses about the most probable structure. He was also very skilled at mentally conceptualizing the physical structure of a molecule.

Not all of his ideas proved correct. During the war years, for example, he had tried to develop a synthetic (not natural; human-made) antibody to combat a type of pneumonia. It would have been the first time that a scientist had created antibodies outside the human body. He did not succeed, but some of his research helped other scientists later on. This was also true of other research Pauling conducted that did not necessarily lead to a new theory or discovery for him.

Once, when a student asked him the best way to get good ideas, Pauling replied, "You must have lots of ideas. Just throw away the bad ones."

James Watson and Francis Crick to figure out the molecular structure of DNA.

With his knowledge of chemical bonds and molecular structure, Linus Pauling was well-situated to solve the DNA-structure puzzle himself. He had worked on the problem off and on for several years, once publishing a proposed three-stranded structure that turned out to be incorrect. This

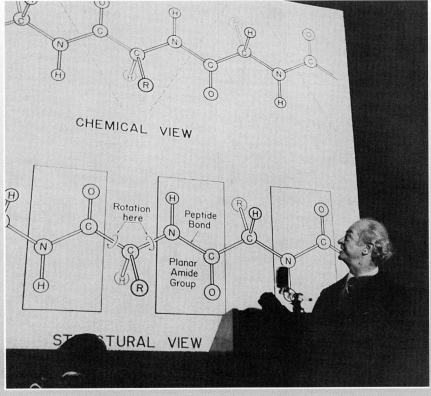

CHEMICAL VIEW

Rotation here

Peptide Bond

Planar Amide Group

STRUCTURAL VIEW

Linus Pauling was a creative scientist and a well-liked teacher.

paper, in fact, was shown to Watson and Crick by Pauling's son Linus, Jr. Many knowledgeable people feel that, had Pauling seen the photos at King's College, as Watson did, Pauling might have figured out the double-helical shape of DNA. Later, Watson and Crick credited Pauling's book on chemical bonding, his use of molecular models, and his alpha-helix theory for helping them to achieve their feat.

New Works in Progress

Frustrated with the State Department restrictions on his travel, Pauling organized a conference in Pasadena. A group of scientists who were working on proteins attended this meeting in September 1953. By that time, Max Perutz had come to accept Pauling's alpha-helix model, so there were no arguments during the discussions. However, there was a great deal of excitement about the April 1953 DNA discovery by Watson and Crick.

Pauling was involved in other pursuits as well. Not all were successes. Often, he did not hesitate to publish findings before he was certain that they were correct. Critics have said that Pauling moved too quickly to take a position and was sometimes overly confident. By the same token, he was secure enough not to fear being wrong. For example, a paper that he published in 1953 on electrons and magnetism was harshly criticized by some colleagues. They attacked his mathematical calculations and his conclusions. They also accused Pauling of making incorrect assumptions about the physical traits of electrons. He received letters pointing out various errors.

Increasing Activism

The year 1953 was turbulent. Pauling was trying to balance research, writing, teaching, and family life. He had to limit some of his activities, such as conferences away from home. In April, however, he very much wanted to go to India in order to attend a conference and observe scientists at work in that country. He and Ava Helen went to New York City primarily for other reasons, but they expected to obtain a passport and travel from there to India. But once again, Pauling found that the State Department had denied him a U.S. passport. Despite his efforts to obtain one, nothing he did worked, and the couple could not go to India. They returned to their home in California, very discouraged by the entire frustrating experience.

While Pauling was still enduring his passport troubles, some of his friends and colleagues also clashed with the federal government. Dr. Thomas Addis, who had treated Pauling for his kidney infections, was harassed by the McCarthy committee. This incident upset Pauling. He believed firmly that the U.S. Constitution permits Americans the right of free association and free expression of their political ideas, whether or not the ideas are popular with everyone. When the doctor's medical practice dwindled because of his damaged reputation, Pauling found Addis a new job in his laboratory.

Robert Oppenheimer, who had headed the Manhattan Project, also found himself under fire by the federal government. The Atomic Energy Commission had decided that, because of his political views, Oppenheimer posed a security risk to the nation. Like Pauling and many others, Oppenheimer had been accused but never convicted of being a Communist. Denying him clearance at this time seemed strange because, years before, he had received security clearance from the Federal Bureau of Investigation (FBI). This clearance allowed Oppenheimer to work on the project that developed the atomic bomb. Pauling joined other scientists and citizens in criticizing the actions taken against Oppenheimer.

A Nobel Laureate

Good news came in the midst of these troubles, in November 1954. While Pauling was delivering a talk on hemoglobin at Cornell University, he was called to the telephone. The students and professors in the hall cheered and applauded when Pauling returned and told them that he had just been notified that he had won the Nobel Prize for Chemistry. The Nobel committee had recognized his work in discovering the structure of proteins and other scientific achievements made over three decades. The medals and prize money would be given to all of the Nobel prize–winners on December 10, in Stockholm, Sweden.

Pauling applied at once for a passport to attend the Nobel prize ceremonies. Days passed with no word from the passport office. Phone calls and letters on Pauling's behalf, along with the importance of the prize itself, must have swayed the passport office in his favor. Some officials, however, still wished to deny him the legal right to go to Sweden. They were overruled, and about two weeks before he was due to depart, Pauling finally received his passport.

At the ceremony, as Ava Helen, Peter, Linda, Crellin, Linus, Jr., and his wife, Anita, looked on, Pauling sat with other Nobel Laureates on the stage of the Royal Concert Hall in Stockholm. Among them were three American scientists who had won the Nobel Prize in Physiology or Medicine. They had developed a new tissue-culturing technique that allowed scientists to grow polioviruses, vital to discovering a vaccine for polio. Pauling's award was given for his discovery of "an important principle in the structure of proteins" that was sure to lead to other key discoveries.

Pauling's whole family went to Stockholm with him
(from left to right): Pauling, Ava Helen, Peter, Crellin,
Linus, Jr., Linda, and Linus, Jr.'s wife, Anita.

Pauling was the key speaker at the ceremony dinner, where he talked of the "futility of war." During that week of parties and celebration, Pauling delivered the traditional Nobel lecture as well. He spoke on the subject of modern structural chemistry. Pauling also took time to talk with Swedish college students about his antinuclear views. The elder Paulings remained in Europe for three months—Linus visiting scientific centers and speaking about his work, Ava Helen giving talks to women's groups that were devoted to world peace.

The Pauling Petition

Despite the problems that his political activism had caused him, Pauling resumed his activities when he returned home. He spoke about the ways in which nuclear testing might threaten living things on Earth. For example, Pauling and others pointed out that people in Norway had experienced health problems as a result of nuclear-weapons tests conducted by the Soviet Union.

By 1957, the Eisenhower administration was working on an agreement with the Soviet Union to end the manufacture of nuclear weapons. But the agreement fell through, and the arms race continued. Other nations were also building and testing nuclear weapons, which increased the amount of radioactive fallout in the atmosphere. Through his own research and by studying the scientific literature, Pauling became convinced that radioactive fallout from the air could remain on Earth for a very long time, affecting not only people living at the time but many future generations.

That year, Pauling urged scientists to sign a petition that he had developed asking for a nuclear test-ban treaty. The petition began by saying, "We urge immediate action for an international agreement to stop testing of all nuclear weapons." It discussed potential health hazards of radiation and how they might affect people all over the world. It also described how mutations of human genes, resulting from radiation, could hurt future generations.

By June 1957, more than 2,500 American scientists had signed the petition, including Herbert J. Muller, who had won a Nobel Prize for his work on mutations caused by X rays. But not all scientists were willing to sign. Some physicists said that there was not yet enough information about radioactive fallout to draw clear conclusions. These were methodical people who wished to gather more facts and information before making public statements.

Pauling also heard from some scientists who strongly opposed nuclear weapons but felt that it was too late to stop them from being built. They believed that there was no way to keep various nations from adding these weapons to their arsenals and that ways must be worked out to prevent them from actually being used.

In July 1957, these U.S. Air Force officers intentionally stood under an atomic explosion. Pauling protested nuclear tests such as this.

Later, about 13,000 scientists from other countries also signed the petition. Caltech students came to the Pauling home to help answer the volumes of mail on the subject that arrived from all over the world. The petition was delivered to the United Nations, but that organization took no action after receiving it.

In 1958, Linus Pauling's first nonscientific book, *No More War!*, was published. In the book, dedicated to Ava Helen, Pauling describes the dangers of nuclear fallout. He uses very specific descriptions, explaining how radioactivity can cause mutations in the body, leading to diseases such as cancer. Other scientists who had worked with radiation as a means of causing changes in cell chromosomes knew this to be true. In addition, a number of the scientists and others who had worked with radioactive materials had contracted different cancers at rates higher than were found among the general population. *No More War!* expresses the hope that the people of the world will find ways to resolve conflicts through "peaceful and rational methods."

Pauling planned to organize a group called Everybody's Committee to Outlaw War, and he hoped for international laws that would ban wars. Some people, however—even those like Einstein who advocated peace—believed that Pauling was overly optimistic in thinking that this was possible.

PUBLIC REACTIONS

Some people still believed that Linus Pauling was a Communist and that his political activism was disloyal to the United States. When he was scheduled to appear as

Pauling's book *No More War!* describes
the dangers of radiation to humans.

a guest lecturer, such objections would sometimes sur-
face; his supporters would have to defend him. He was
also attacked by U.S. government leaders for being naive
and inexperienced in world affairs and political decision

making. Mounting criticism at Caltech made it more uncomfortable for Pauling to work there. In 1958, he resigned as chairman of the chemistry department and director of the chemistry labs, although he remained an active member of the faculty until 1963.

Pauling still felt that he must warn the public about the dangers of nuclear testing. On television, Pauling debated physicist Edward Teller, who believed that nuclear superiority was the way to bring a lasting peace. Teller expressed respect for Pauling's scientific work but disagreed with his point of view on the nuclear issue. Those who saw the debate praised Pauling's skill in getting his points across clearly and forcefully.

Pauling developed a friendlier relationship with the physician Albert Schweitzer. The Paulings visited him at his mission hospital in Africa in 1959. Pauling was impressed by Schweitzer's reverence for all forms of life and later mentioned him in some of his speeches. In 1961, Schweitzer worked with Pauling to sponsor a peace conference in Oslo, Norway.

New Troubles

By the 1960s, Linus and Ava Helen were spending more and more time at their ranch in Big Sur, California, which featured a rustic two-room cabin with no telephone or electricity. The Paulings had bought Deer Flat Ranch in 1956, using the Nobel prize money they received that year. The ranch included 122 acres of land near the Pacific Ocean.

In February 1960, Pauling gave his family a scare when he almost died of exposure. Out hiking alone in Big Sur,

Pauling smiled after being rescued from a narrow ledge high above the sea near his Big Sur ranch.

he tumbled over the side of a cliff. Unable to move without falling, he stayed put until sheriff's deputies and bloodhounds found him about 24 hours later.

Pauling needed a rest, not only because of the accident, but as a result of overwork. Yet he found himself under investigation by the government again, and he was called to appear before the Senate Internal Security Committee in June 1960. Ava Helen was especially annoyed at this investigation of her husband. This time, the committee asked him about his 1958 petition calling for a treaty banning nuclear testing. It demanded that he give the names of all those on the petition as well as anyone else who had helped him to gather signatures. Pauling pointed out that the committee already had the names on the petition, and he refused to give them any other names. He said that he would go to jail rather than hurt people who had helped assemble the petition. Although the committee was sharply critical, Pauling's courageous stand brought him support from numerous writers and editors throughout America.

As he had in the past, Pauling spoke to the press to bring public attention to these activities. He said that such committees reduced citizens' rights given by the U.S. Constitution and Bill of Rights. The committee, in turn, called Pauling's behavior "discourteous and defiant." Pauling appeared in front of the committee again in October. This time, a number of spectators were present. They applauded as he argued against the demands of the committee, which did not subpoena him to return.

Not willing to give up his political activity, Pauling launched a new petition effort to stop the manufacture and testing of nuclear weapons. Tired of personal attacks, he sued a newspaper for libel after it called him "anti-American."

VISITING THE WHITE HOUSE

In January 1962, President John F. Kennedy and his wife Jacqueline held a special dinner for 50 Americans who had won the Nobel prize. That same day, there was a "Ban the Bomb" demonstration outside the White House. The Paulings attended both events.

Some politicians, including Arizona senator Barry Goldwater, said that Pauling should be excluded from the

People against nuclear testing marched outside the White House in January 1962. Pauling was the only demonstrator to later have dinner with the President.

dinner, in view of his protests against government policies. Yet Pauling later said that President Kennedy had been good-humored as he greeted the Paulings in the reception line, encouraging Linus to continue to speak up about his beliefs. The First Lady reportedly said that, when the Kennedys' five-year-old daughter, Caroline, had seen Linus Pauling outside, demonstrating, she had asked her mother, "What has Daddy done wrong now?"

Pauling may be the only American who ever crossed his own picket line to attend a White House dinner party made up of famous scientists and political leaders. The years to come would find him involved in still more political and scientific controversies, while achieving yet another historic distinction.

"A FIRST-CLASS GENIUS"

October 10, 1963, was surely one of the most remarkable days in the remarkable life of Linus Pauling. On that day, President John F. Kennedy signed a limited nuclear test-ban treaty with Great Britain and the Soviet Union. On that very same day, Pauling heard that he was to receive his second Nobel—this time the Nobel Peace Prize.

Pauling's daughter, Linda Pauling Kamb, was the first one to be notified about her father's second Nobel prize. Her parents were in Big Sur and could not be reached by telephone. Linda contacted the Forestry Service, and a ranger took the Paulings to a telephone where they could receive the happy news.

Along with many good wishes from friends and colleagues came some inevitable criticism about Pauling being given the prestigious award. Perhaps one of the strongest attacks on the Nobel committee's decision came from *Life* magazine, which entitled its editorial on the subject, "A Weird Insult from Norway."

Stung by criticism from some members of the American Chemical Society, Pauling resigned his membership. He may also have been hurt that the chemistry department at Caltech did not hold an official reception in honor of the award, while the biology division did.

HOPES FOR WORLD PEACE

In receiving the Nobel Peace Prize, Pauling became the only person in history to win two Nobel prizes that were both unshared with others. At this, Pauling's second Nobel ceremony, held in Oslo, Norway, his accompanying family included a grandson, Linus III, as well. As the award was presented, Pauling was praised for his sense of ethical responsibility and for his ongoing fight against nuclear weapons. The committee expressed appreciation that Pauling was combining the work of science with the pursuit of human ideals.

During his Nobel lecture, Pauling spoke hopefully of a world without war—"a world characterized by economic, political, and social justice for all human beings, and a culture worthy of man's intelligence."

Although Pauling expressed the hope that his Nobel Peace Prize would make it "respectable to work for peace," criticism of his political activities continued. And, at

The chairman of the Norwegian committee (left) presented
Pauling with his second Nobel prize in 1963.

Caltech, he was told that his research space was going to
be reduced. Some of his colleagues believed that his new
research ideas, centered on brain chemistry, seemed poorly
thought-out. For these and other reasons, Pauling decided
to leave Caltech, after some 40 years of studying, teaching,
and working at that institution.

Linus Pauling

Studying Brain Chemistry

Seeking a more open environment, Pauling decided to go to the Center for the Study of Democratic Institutions, a facility 100 miles up the coast from Pasadena, in Santa Barbara, California. Santa Barbara was closer to Deer Flat Ranch, where the Paulings had built a larger home. There, they enjoyed visits from their children and grandchildren. The home included two studies, one for Linus and one for Ava Helen. Both overlooked the ocean.

Pauling officially resigned from Caltech on June 30, 1964, but he decided to retain the title "research associate," keeping this tie to the institute. Because his new setting was a "think-tank," an institution devoted to analyzing political issues and government policies, Pauling would be able to pursue those interests more freely.

Yet there were no scientific facilities at the Center for the Study of Democratic Institutions. Pauling remained there only three years. They were quiet years, ones marked by few publications.

Pauling's mind had been at work, however, on a subject that had intrigued him since the late 1950s. At that time, Pauling had begun wondering about brain chemistry and possible links among chemicals, nutrition, and mental illness. Having studied proteins, he considered ways in which he might investigate cells in the brain. Studying these cells posed new challenges, because the biochemistry of the brain is very complex and difficult to gain access to.

His interest in the biological aspects of mental disease put Linus Pauling squarely against the majority views of the time. He was the first prominent scientist to state that the

"A First-Class Genius"

A discarded molecular model decorated the
Paulings' Santa Barbara home in the mid-1960s.

biochemical environment of the brain is vital to its functioning and that disturbances in this biochemistry might result in symptoms of illness in various individuals.

During the 1950s, most people believed that mental problems were psychologically based—that is, they arose from the way a person developed and was treated by others in the environment while growing up. Psychologists used "talk therapy" or behavioral approaches to treat people with mental illnesses.

In recent years, there has been far more emphasis on the impact of chemical imbalances and nutrition on mental disorders. Sophisticated technology has enabled scientists to examine brain tissue, blood, and other body chemistry for

Linus Pauling

subtle imbalances. Scientists have discovered differences between the brains and nerve cells of normal people and those diagnosed with schizophrenia or other major mental illnesses. Pauling is now regarded as a pioneer in this effort.

But during the 1960s, as Pauling first suggested these possibilities, many critics regarded him as eccentric, or worse.

Thirty years ago, high-tech brain scans such as this one were not possible. Pauling was one of the first to consider the connection between brain chemistry and mental disorders.

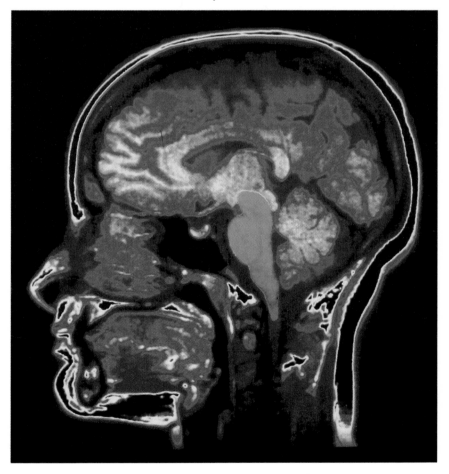

"A First-Class Genius"

When Pauling's research led him to conclude that niacin (vitamin B-3) is essential for a healthy nervous system, members of the medical community scoffed and said that he lacked credentials in the fields of nutrition or medicine. This criticism would often be leveled against him in years to come.

An Orthomolecular Approach to Health

As usual, Pauling did not dodge controversy but continued to explore his ideas. Eager to resume laboratory research and teaching, he joined the faculty of the University of California at San Diego in 1967.

Now 66 years old, Pauling was developing an approach to the treatment of disease called "orthomolecular medicine"—from the Greek word *ortho*, which means "correct," and the word *molecular*, referring to "molecules." In his view, the chemistry of the body cells, organs, and systems will be in healthy balance when the right molecules are located in the right places in the right amounts.

The academic surroundings in San Diego produced exciting work from Pauling. He wrote scientific papers about orthomolecular psychiatry, again sparking mixed reactions. In one paper, Pauling discussed how orthomolecular therapy might be used to treat certain mental diseases. Working with a talented former student, Arthur Robinson, who was now a professor at the university, Pauling began vitamin studies. Among other things, Pauling and Robinson analyzed the vitamin content of urine specimens taken from people diagnosed with mental diseases and those considered to be mentally healthy.

New Honors

In 1969, Pauling took a new job once again: He was named professor emeritus (an honorary title) at Stanford University in Palo Alto, California, near San Francisco. In this position, Pauling consulted with other professors rather than teaching classes of his own. Despite the criticism that Pauling had received over some of his new theories, he had continued to be given recognition for his achievements. In 1971, Graham Chedd, a science writer for *New Scientist* magazine, called Pauling "arguably the greatest scientist alive today." The readers of this respected British journal ranked Pauling as one of the most important scientists of all time. Pauling received the first Dr. Martin Luther King, Jr., Medical Achievement Award, in 1972. The award honored his groundbreaking work on sickle-cell anemia.

One of Pauling's dreams came true that same year when his Linus Pauling Institute of Science and Medicine was set up in Palo Alto. Later, it would move to a building in nearby Menlo Park. (After his death, it found a permanent home under the direction of his son Linus, Jr., in Corvallis, Oregon, connected to Oregon State University.) Both the Linus Pauling Institute and Stanford were close to Big Sur, where Pauling and Ava Helen now lived full-time on their ranch. Pauling enjoyed spending time outdoors and working quietly alone. In the peace and quiet of his surroundings, he seemed to generate some of the finest ideas of his later years. He also began to see his role as that of encouraging and stimulating young students.

Pauling was still politically active, but he worried less about nuclear war. The worst of the Cold War tensions between the United States and the Soviet Union were over. He continued to urge peaceful relations among nations and warned that biological hazards could result from the peacetime uses of nuclear energy. Pauling was not alone. By now, prominent American research laboratories had also concluded that exposure to high levels of radiation could lead to birth defects and cancers.

In the meantime, the Committee on Internal Security, part of the U.S. House of Representatives, had finally concluded that Pauling was not a Communist or a threat to the nation. He received the National Medal of Science in 1975, after years of being nominated and then rejected for political reasons. President Gerald Ford authorized the award, citing Pauling's "extraordinary power and scope of his imagination which has led to basic contributions in such diverse fields as structural chemistry and the nature of genetic diseases." Linus and Ava Helen also enjoyed a festive, very well-attended party at Caltech in 1976, held in honor of his 75th birthday.

THE DEBATE OVER VITAMIN C

The early 1970s had found Pauling immersed in studies of vitamin C (ascorbic acid). He tried to publish articles stating that increased doses of vitamin C might reduce colds. *The Proceedings of the National Academy* refused the articles, although Pauling had been a member since the 1930s. This happened again in 1991, when he submitted an article about vitamin C and heart disease. The academy reasoned that such articles might "harm the public welfare." Pauling's article was published in another journal.

In the 1970s, Pauling studied the connection between disease prevention and vitamin C, shown here in an enhanced microphotograph.

Pauling continued to share his unorthodox ideas about vitamins. In 1976, he recommended that adults take one or more grams (1,000 milligrams or more) of vitamin C a day. He pointed out that humans do not make this vitamin in their bodies, as almost all other animals do, so it must be supplied through food and supplements on a regular basis. He himself began taking 1,000 to 3,000 milligrams of the vitamin daily. (The recommended daily allowance, as specified by the U.S. Food and Drug Agency, is only 60 milligrams per day for adults.)

He continued to review all the available literature about vitamin C, and during 1978 and 1979, he and Dr. Ewan

Cameron studied cancer patients in Scotland. They found that the survival time was four times longer in patients who received large doses of vitamin C.

The scientific and medical communities continued to scoff at these ideas. To reach the general public, Pauling wrote his books *Cancer and Vitamin C* (with Dr. Ewan Cameron) and *How to Live Longer and Feel Better.* He appeared on numerous talk shows to discuss his ideas.

In later years, Linus Pauling would take what is called a megadose—2,000 to 18,000 milligrams a day—of vitamin C. He contended in 1993 that vitamin C could help to protect people from virtually all diseases. By the 1990s, millions of people around the world were taking extra vitamin C to ward off various diseases.

Thousands of scientific papers done since the early 1970s have supported Pauling's claim that higher than usual amounts of vitamin C can benefit human health. Some studies show that vitamin C counteracts the carcinogenic, or cancer-producing, effects of nitrites in foods. (Nitrites are often used in food as preservatives.) Vitamin C is also one of the antioxidants—chemicals that work in the body to neutralize free radicals, chemicals that may promote cancer. Researchers think that vitamin C also helps to stabilize cholesterol in the blood, which prevents it from hardening in the blood vessels.

In May 1992, epidemiologist (one who studies disease) James Enstrom reported an experiment that supported Pauling's idea that people who consumed more vitamin C through supplements and food lived longer. He studied 11,000 Americans and found that men who had at least 300 milligrams of vitamin C a day lived up to six years longer than those who took in less.

In 1979, Pauling became the first person to receive the U.S. National Academy of Sciences Medal in the Chemical Sciences. The Irish government gave Pauling its Celtic Medal, in recognition of his efforts "in defending the rights of the world's children and for his innovative work in preparing a better future for mankind."

A TERRIBLE LOSS

Meanwhile, Pauling faced the most tragic event in his life. Ava Helen was dying of cancer. Although exhausted and ill, she continued working for causes she believed in. During the months before she died, in December 1981, she lectured about the issues she held most dear: equality and nuclear disarmament. The Ava Helen Pauling Lectureship for World Peace at Oregon State University was eventually established in her honor.

Pauling found some comfort in his work and continued to study scientific problems. He returned more than once to examine the chemical bond as it applied to various problems in structural chemistry. Sometimes he sent letters or articles to scientific journals as thoughts and questions occurred to him. He proposed a way of applying his chemical-bond theories to superconductivity (the increase in electrical conductivity, or movement, of materials when they are at extremely low temperatures). Later, a well-known physicist, P. W. Anderson of Princeton University, said that Pauling's papers on chemical bonding had helped his research in superconductivity. Researchers at the Linus Pauling Institute were also investigating a variety of subjects, including cancer, AIDS, and viruses.

This "floating" magnet shows that the material below it is in a superconducting state. Pauling thought that his chemical-bond theories could apply to superconductors.

Busy Last Years

During the 1980s, Linus Pauling made more television appearances and lectured around the country. White-haired, often wearing his trademark beret, he discussed his theories about vitamins, environmental medicine, and orthomolecular medicine. Although he now avoided most large social gatherings, he attended the 85th birthday party that Caltech held in his honor.

In 1989, Pauling won yet another award, the Vannevar Bush Prize from the National Science Foundation. Yet the foundation refused his request for a grant that would have financed a new computer and assistant. Of this and other experiences, Pauling suggested that scientists who pursue original theories find it harder than more conventional scientists to get their papers published and to get grants.

Linus Pauling remained active and involved in science during the last years of his life. He was healthy and vigorous. At home, he typically rose before dawn and worked through the afternoon, writing papers and letters, reading science journals, and making calculations. In one letter to an editor, written in 1994, a few months before his death, Pauling challenged the conclusions in a paper that had appeared in *Science* magazine. He analyzed the findings about the crystal structure of a compound and said that the relative strength of certain bonds might be different from those reported by the other scientist. His specific formulas and explanations showed a sharp and curious mind.

Pauling was still hard at work in December 1992, when this photo was taken.

Linus Pauling's leisure activities included spending time with his children, grandchildren, and great-grandchildren. He liked to read science fiction and told interviewers that he watched the evening news.

A Rich Legacy

Linus Carl Pauling died of prostate cancer on August 19, 1994, at his home in Big Sur. Tributes to the 93-year-old scientist appeared in newspapers throughout the world. Journalists noted his scientific exploits, personal charisma, and humanitarian concerns. *The New York Times* quoted Pauling as saying that all citizens should work to make the world a place "in which every person who is born will have the opportunity to lead a good life."

Summing up his traits, writers and scientists commented that Linus Pauling was both a scientist and a humanist, combining great intellect with true social concern. His discoveries advanced many older fields of science and helped to develop new ones, affecting science in profound ways. More than anyone else, Desmond Bernal noted, Linus Pauling spread the knowledge of quantum theory to students of chemistry.

Pauling also laid the groundwork for genetic research, and his work on chemical bonds and proteins led to many new medications. His research on blood and hemoglobin led to new understanding of several diseases besides sickle-cell anemia. The growth of environmental medicine and the use of nutrition and vitamins to treat disease also owe much to Pauling. He gave these fields of scientific study a greater level of legitimacy.

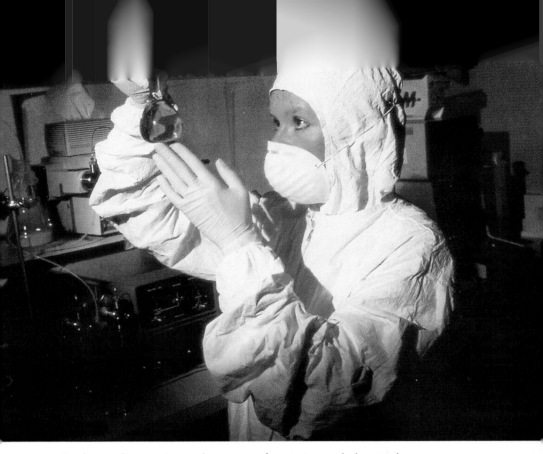

Pauling's discoveries in the areas of proteins and chemical bonds helped make possible many types of today's medical research, such as this work on artificial ligaments.

In addition, Linus Pauling the teacher prepared future generations of new scientists who have gone on to their own important work and who have taught many others. Scientist and writer Isaac Asimov expressed the thoughts of many when he called Pauling "a first-class genius." And James Watson, another important scientist who was inspired by Pauling, called him "the greatest of all chemists."

Through his courage, curiosity, and determined effort, Linus Pauling left behind a scientific and humanitarian legacy that has not been surpassed by any other twentieth-century scientist.

Glossary

amino acid One of the 20 naturally occurring molecules containing carbon, nitrogen, oxygen, and hydrogen in a specific arrangement that allows them to bond together in a long chain; the building blocks of protein molecules.

atom A minute particle that makes up a chemical element; the smallest particle that retains the properties of the element.

biology The study of living organisms.

chemical bonding The process by which atoms join together to form molecules.

chemistry The study of the composition, structure, and traits of matter.

chromosomes Long, coiled, threadlike material— consisting mostly of DNA and proteins—that stores genetic information, found in the cells of living things and in viruses.

crystal A solid in which all the components (atoms, molecules) are arranged in a regular, orderly fashion.

DNA (deoxyribonucleic acid) A substance that is found in the cells of living things and viruses that carries genetic information from a parent organism to its offspring.

electron A subatomic particle with a negative charge.

gene A unit of a chromosome that contains a single trait that is passed on through inheritance; usually one gene has the code for one protein.

genetics The study of heredity—how traits are passed on from one generation to another.

helix An object that takes the shape of a spiral.

hemoglobin A substance found in red blood cells that carries oxygen throughout the body.

inorganic Describes matter that is not organic.

molecule The smallest fragment of a compound that retains all the properties of that substance.

organic Describes matter that is composed of carbon, along with hydrogen and other non-metallic elements.

physics The branch of science that studies matter, energy, and the interactions between them.

protein A class of large molecules made up of amino acids, whose members are vital components of most biological tissues, including those for blood, hair, skin, and muscles, and that participate in nearly all metabolic processes.

quantum mechanics A branch of physics that studies the physical forces that give atoms their properties and hold them together in molecules.

resonance An aspect of quantum mechanics that states that the true (complex) structure of a molecule can be described by a special mathematical sum of several individual (simple) structures.

sickle-cell anemia (sickle-cell disease) An inherited condition in which most of the red blood cells are an abnormal crescent (sickle) shape, reducing ability to carry oxygen throughout the body.

valence The number of bonds that an atom can form, determined by the number of electrons and the way in which they are arranged.

X-ray crystallography A technique used to analyze chemical structure by aiming X rays through slides containing crystallized molecules, then recording those rays on photographic film.

Further Reading

Aaseng, Nathan. *Peace Seekers: The Nobel Peace Prize.*
   Minneapolis, MN: Lerner, 1991.
Asimov, Isaac. *How Did We Find Out About DNA?*
   New York: Walker and Company, 1985.
Barber, Jacqueline. *Vitamin C Testing.* Berkeley, CA:
   Lawrence Science, 1990.
Newton, David. *Linus Pauling: Scientist and Advocate.*
   New York: Facts On File, 1995.
Sherrow, Victoria. *Watson and Crick.* Woodbridge, CT:
   Blackbirch Press, 1995.
White, Florence Meiman. *Linus Pauling: Scientist and
   Crusader.* New York: Walker and Company, 1980.

Sources

Asimov, Isaac. *Asimov's Biographical Encyclopedia of Science and
   Technology.* New York: Doubleday, 1982.
Atkins, P. W. *Molecules.* New York: Scientific American Library, 1987.
"A Weird Insult from Norway." *Life,* October 25, 1963, p. 4.
Baskin, Yvonne. *The Gene Doctors: Medical Genetics at the Frontier.*
   New York: William Morrow, 1984.
Buckley, William. "Are You Being Sued by Linus Pauling?" *National
   Review,* September 25, 1962, p. 218.
Carroll, Jerry. "The Perils of Pauling." *New West,* October 8, 1979.
Carter, Luther J. "Pauling Gets Medal of Science: Thaw Between
   Scientists and the White House." *Science,* October 3, 1975, p. 30.
Cousins, Norman. "Linus Pauling and the Vitamin Controversy,"
   Saturday Review, May 15, 1971, pp. 37, 44.
Crick, Francis. *Of Molecules and Men.* Seattle: University of Washington
   Press, 1966.

———. *What Mad Pursuit?* New York: Basic Books, 1988.

Fry, William F., Jr. "What's New with You, Linus Pauling?" *The Humanist*, November–December 1974, p. 17.

Gleick, Elizabeth. "Linus Pauling Scientist," *People*, September 5, 1994, p. 69.

Grosser, Morton. "Linus Pauling: Molecular Artist." *The Saturday Evening Post*, Fall 1971, p. 14.

Kalven, Harry, Jr. "Congressional Testing of Linus Pauling." *The Bulletin of the Atomic Scientists*, December 1960.

"Linus Pauling." *Scientific American*, November 1931, p. 293.

"Linus Pauling TKO." *National Review*, May 3, 1966, p. 403.

Olby, Robert. *The Path to the Double Helix*. Seattle: University of Washington Press, 1974.

O'Neil, Paul. "The Vitamin C Mania." *Life*, July 9, 1971, p. 130.

"Pauling and the Senate Committee," *Science*, October 14, 1960, p. 1001.

Pauling, Linus. *Cancer and Vitamin C*. New York: Warner, 1979.

Pauling, Linus. Nobel Prize in Peace Award Address, 1963.

———. *No More War!* New York: Dodd, Mead, 1958.

———. "Of Mice and Men." *Barron's*, June 11, 1979.

———. "Orthomolecular Psychiatry." *Science*, April 19, 1968, pp. 265–271.

———. "The Social Responsibilities of Scientists." *The Science Teacher*, May 1966, p. 17.

———. "The Wonders of Vitamin C." *Muscle and Fitness*, February 1994, pp. 130ff.

Pauling, Linus, and Cameron, Ewan. "Modern Structural Chemistry," in Weaver, Jefferson Hame. *The World of Physics, Vol. II*, pp. 530–541. New York: Simon and Schuster, 1987.

"The Prize Winner: Linus Pauling Believed in the Moral Duty of Scientists." *People*, September 5, 1994, p. 69.

Report of the Subcommittee to Investigate the Administration of the Internal Security Act and Other Internal Security Laws to the Committee on the Judiciary: U.S. Senate, 87th Congress 1st Session. "Testimony of Linus Pauling," June 21, and October 11, 1960, p. 5.

Sayer, Anne. *Rosalind Franklin and DNA*. New York: W. W. Norton, 1975.

Serafini, Anthony. *Linus Pauling: A Man and His Science*. New York: Paragon House, 1989.

Strout, Richard. "Win a Prize; Get a Passport." *Life*, November 28, 1955.

Watson, James Dewey. *The Double Helix*. New York: Atheneum, 1968.

INDEX

Boldfaced, italicized page numbers include picture references.

Photo Credits
Cover (background): ©Irving Geis/Science Source/Photo Researchers,
Inc.; cover (inset) and pages 25, 31, 38, 57, 63, 71, 81, 83, 85, 87, 89, 92, 94:
AP/Wide World Photos, Inc.; pages 4, 28, 77: California Institute of Tech-
nology; page 41: ©P. M. Motta & S. Correr/Science Photo Library/Photo
Researchers, Inc.; page 75: ©Kenneth Eward/BioGrafx/Science Source/
Photo Researchers, Inc.; page 95: ©Scott Camazine/Photo Researchers,
Inc.; page 99: ©Alfred Pasieka/Science Photo Library/Photo Researchers,
Inc.; page 102: ©Photo Researchers, Inc.; page 103: ©Michael Schumann/
SABA; page 105: ©Doug Menuez/SABA
Graphics by Blackbirch Graphics, Inc.